# SEIKI JUTSU

"This text is in the tradition of great memoirs of spiritual discovery like those of Lama Govinda, Carl Jung, and Gurdjieff. . . . The teaching of seiki jutsu itself is yet again one of those radically simple openings to the real—the reminder we always need to return again and again to our origins."

DON HANLON JOHNSON, PH.D., FOUNDER OF THE SOMATIC PSYCHOLOGY PROGRAM AT CALIFORNIA INSTITUTE OF INTEGRAL STUDIES AND AUTHOR OF *BODY, SPIRIT, AND DEMOCRACY*

"We thank the Keeneys for their introduction of seiki jutsu to the healing arts. Their way of tapping in to the Dreaming brings creativity to spirituality and healing. We love the direction of this teaching!"

AMY AND ARNOLD MINDELL, PH.D., DEVELOPERS OF "PROCESS ORIENTED PSYCHOLOGY" AND AUTHORS OF *RIDING THE HORSE BACKWARDS*

"Bradford and Hillary Keeney are bold explorers investigating the world's rich tradition of healing arts. With deep respect and awe for the cultures they visit, the two of them bring back wisdom and practical methods of boosting our health, happiness, and sense of meaning. Their latest subject is seiki jutsu, a powerful form of movement therapy and energy work that looks promising as a way to alleviate some of the problems of our increasingly fragmented and sedentary lives."

JAY WALLJASPER, FORMER EDITORIAL DIRECTOR AND EDITOR OF *UTNE READER,* AND AUTHOR OF *ALL THAT WE SHARE: A FIELD GUIDE TO THE COMMONS*

# SEIKI JUTSU

## The Practice of
## Non-Subtle Energy Medicine

BRADFORD AND HILLARY KEENEY

Healing Arts Press
Rochester, Vermont • Toronto, Canada

Healing Arts Press
One Park Street
Rochester, Vermont 05767
www.HealingArtsPress.com

Text stock is SFI certified

Healing Arts Press is a division of Inner Traditions International

***Note to the reader:*** *This book is intended as an informational guide. The remedies,
approaches, and techniques described herein are meant to supplement, and not to be a
substitute for, professional medical care or treatment. They should not be used to treat
a serious ailment without prior consultation with a qualified health care professional.*

**Library of Congress Cataloging-in-Publication Data**

Keeney, Bradford, 1951– author.
  Seiki jutsu : the practice of non-subtle energy medicine / Bradford Keeney and
Hillary Keeney.
     pages cm
  Includes bibliographical references and index.
  ISBN 978-1-62055-234-6 (pbk.) — ISBN 978-1-62055-253-7 (e-book)
  1. Energy medicine. 2. Mental healing. I. Keeney, Hillary, author. II. Title.
  RZ421.K44 2014
  615.8'51—dc23

                                                                2013037044

Printed and bound in the United States by Lake Book Manufacturing, Inc.
The text stock is SFI certified. The Sustainable Forestry Initiative® program
promotes sustainable forest management.

10 9 8 7 6 5 4 3 2 1

Text design by Priscilla Baker and layout by Brian Boynton
This book was typeset in Garamond Premier Pro with Swiss 721 and Warnock
Pro as display typefaces.

To send correspondence to the author of this book, mail a first-class letter to the
author c/o Inner Traditions • Bear & Company, One Park Street, Rochester, VT
05767, and we will forward the communication, or contact the author directly at
**www.keeneyinstitute.org**.

# CONTENTS

# 1

# INTRODUCTION TO SEIKI

Rocking back and forth, we celebrate one of the world's oldest self-healing, rejuvenation, and spiritual practices. It requires no particular belief, understanding, or elaborate explanation and is available to anyone who is both courageous and childlike enough to do something so simple. Its basic principle can be articulated with these two words: Do nothing. If you have to think about what this means, you will miss its instruction. This is an invitation to plunge into spontaneity.

Moved by a strong, invisible current, we feel a dynamic, tingling energy throughout our bodies. It matters not what this experience is called or how any spiritual, philosophical, or scientific theory attempts to explain it. We are content and satisfied to feel it and be moved, letting go of all contrived habits that try to make life happen.

Even if you have just one authentic experience of being inside this current—really inside it—it is enough to transform your whole being. Falling deeper into the current without effort, the desire for power and control falls away. "Pow" and "kapow" are let go in favor of "be-here-now Tao." Words now prefer flowing inside improvisation. The words, like you, want to be set free.

Jump into the river of seiki. You'll know it when you're there, for you will bob like a cork on water and rock back and forth like a baby held by its mother in a rocking chair. Stay there longer. Watch how other spontaneous movements spring forth. They are fascinating and will catch you by surprise—suddenly your interest in the performance of an effortless, moving, changing you is far more interesting than old habits of thinking.

Become enveloped by the current that has no need for the effort of mindful attention. Get out of the way and let life make you happen; allow life's wondrous movement to grab hold of you and carry you along with it. Be distracted by life: distraction rather than attraction is the secret. Your mind will lose track of how you are able to constantly change. It's exhilarating, renewing, even intoxicating.

Hold our hands and feel where the current takes us. Are you feeling a tidal wave of heat flowing from the top of your head to the bottom of your soles? Or is it flowing from the bottom to the top? Anything can be experienced inside this stream—anything except tiredness, sickness, worry, jealousy, hatred, malaise, loneliness, and discontent. The deeper you plunge, the stronger you feel deep empathy, connection, joy, and love. Let the motion be inseparable from this exalted emotion. Feel free to celebrate with all kinds of commotion! We are. Shout out praise and joy! The universe dances and sings inside of you.

It's incredible what happens, isn't it? The more you

offer praise, the happier you become. You are feeding joy with joy. The celebration of life is returned with more life. This is how it has always been, though we have forgotten. Don't analyze—go deeper and further into the stream. There you can only laugh and love. If you remain on the riverbank, you risk getting all dried up. That's the aging you want to avoid. The fountain of youth is found inside the current of the flowing stream. Enter the timelessness that is always present for all ages.

One of the oldest cultures in the world, the Kalahari Bushmen, lives inside this holy river, even though they make their home in a vast desert. The samurai of ancient Japan knew how to swim inside this fluidic spontaneity, even though they appeared to have extraordinary control. Their secret is found in the constant natural movements of a child. Bobbing, rocking, swaying, and dancing, children are constantly moving. When they stop, largely because parents and teachers command them to sit still and stop fidgeting, their energy drains away. School becomes an impossible exercise of trying to stay awake. Do you remember? Unless you were totally engrossed in a project, the more quiet and still you became at your desk, the more likely you were to doze off into slumber. But when the bell rang you ran to the playground, full of instant energy. Where did that burst of aliveness come from?

The bell is ringing for you now.

Move and the world moves with you. Move and notice you are the change. Move and find that inspired words flow like poetry. Move and feel moved to love. The alternative is sitting still and drowning in the internal recycled chatter that tries to figure out how to get on board the ship to glory, the train to success, the flight to happiness. But you are already on it! Once you know that, you will feel the current inside and outside of you. You'll find happy feet and a joyful voice. It will be impossible not to experience the thrill of being alive, even if you have only a day to live.

Welcome to seiki, the old Japanese word for the vital life force. We refer to it as the non-subtle life force because experiencing it is unquestionably obvious and so powerful that it can transform your life in an instant. If you wonder whether you have experienced seiki, you haven't. Once you have met seiki, you know it and never forget it. Seiki invites you to take a stand for your life. It inspires you to jump—even take a somersault—for life! You deserve to feel alive and to be exhilarated, lightened, and transformed, unrestrained by sideline commentary of the interpreting mind. Move right now! Shout out loud: "Yes!" Have you ever shouted a whisper? Shout a whisper as loudly as you can: "Yes! Yes! Yes!" Say yes to life and life will notice. It will rush inside of you and be instantly ready to take you on an extraordinary ride— the journey of a life recharged with seiki, the miraculous and ever delightful non-subtle vital life force.

---

The key to achieving a happy, meaningful, and fulfilled life is found in your relationship with seiki. When you are filled with seiki, you are able to mobilize well-being, awaken creative expression, and optimize every-day performance. We introduce you to the Japanese practice of seiki jutsu, the art of the non-subtle vital life force. Seiki makes you feel as alive as you can possibly feel.

Ikuko Osumi Sensei, one of the greatest practitioners of seiki jutsu, described seiki as "activated and strengthened ki," made ready for empowered transmission and reception by human beings. Seiki is enhanced, concentrated, and supercharged life force. The practice of cultivating your connection with seiki is one of the most valuable gifts you can give yourself. Seiki jutsu enables you to encounter your true nature, and to be continually tuned and recharged to carry out your unique destiny.

People talk about "energy" all the time. We mention energy when we refer to the essential quality of a person, relationship, performance, situation, thing, or place.

> "I like her energy."
> "This place has exceptional energy."
> "He drains my energy."
> "She has charismatic energy."
> "That music energizes me."
> "This painting has good energy."

We like and dislike certain energies; we recognize good, bad, unusual, special, low, neutral, or high energy. But what do we really mean when we use this term, other than its being a comment regarding how we feel about something?

Scientifically speaking, energy is all there is. When Albert Einstein suggested that what we call matter is only energy that is moving slowly enough for us to perceive it as solid, this applies to us as well. Our brain, heart, guts, and skin are composed of electromagnetic forces in motion, all moving at incredible speed. The patterns of energy in our whole being determine the quality of our life. Our well-being is a consequence of our energetics, the vital life force or seiki that resides and circulates within.

When a musical performance carries the energized emotion to pierce your heart and soul, you know you're in the presence of activated energy. Simply going through the motions with mere technique alone cannot enliven music. Whether it be art, sport, cooking, or everyday living, we desire our expression to be fully alive and charged with positive energy. Seiki is the current, vibe, and energy from which life flows. With seiki jutsu, you have the know-how to bring forth an energized life. Heart and soul will only arise when seiki is thriving within you.

Seiki jutsu is a unique self-healing, revitalization, and spiritual practice based on spontaneous expression. The transformative art of handling seiki, the vital life force, consists of:

1. transmitting enhanced seiki
2. a daily practice for its development, and
3. healing modalities that address body movement and therapeutic conversation.

Seiki jutsu differs from other movement-based practices in that it emphasizes spontaneity over choreographed form. Unlike most bodywork and energy-oriented therapeutic methods, seiki jutsu has no prescribed movements, preferred choreographies, or elaborate explanatory systems. It proposes that the spontaneous, natural movements of the body deliver and infuse its basic teaching and that, over time, the performance of these movements results in resourceful outcomes for the practitioner.

In 1928, Jozo Ishii of the Seiki Ryoho Kenkyu Jo (Seiki Treatment Institute and Research Establishment) in Japan published a book entitled "Essentials of Seiki Self-Healing Therapy," arguably the first written account of seiki jutsu. Ishii reported research on how seiki jutsu could resolve body disorders, ward off illness, revitalize well-being, and promote longevity. Japanese practitioners have referred to it as the fountain of youth. It was also claimed to awaken and nurture creative talent and spiritual gifts. Some translated excerpts of this source text are published in this book as an appendix.

Seiki jutsu was well established centuries before reiki was developed and was used by the samurai. It is thought to have existed in the early times of Shintoism, perhaps as far back as the eighth century, and holds within it ancient Japanese shamanic ways of handling the life force. In addition to being a self-help practice, seiki jutsu is a healing modality that emphasizes hands-on interaction—skin-to-skin contact—and its experience leaves no doubt as to its presence. Seiki jutsu practitioners experience a wide range of electric-like sensations, from vibratory buzzing to strong convulsing waves throughout their bodies.

Don Wright, former teacher of Ericksonian hypnotherapy at the Esalen Institute and aikido practitioner, describes his first experience of seiki, which was administered by Bradford Keeney: "I felt like I was floating and wanted to move my body with speed and precision. All of my senses were intensified. I recognized this condition as being similar to the ki activation that I had learned to utilize in aikido training. The difference was that the intensity of this energy was magnitudes beyond what I had previously experienced; it was beyond what I'd ever imagined."[1]

The following chapter, "Ikuko Osumi Sensei and the Lineage of Seiki Jutsu," presents the foremost practitioner and master of seiki jutsu in the twentieth century. Ikuko Osumi Sensei received seiki from her aunt in 1935. Ikuko Osumi was spiritually inspired by stories about her ancestor from the 1600s, Eizon Hoin, who revived a shrine on Mt. Maki and was reportedly responsible for numerous miracles. Today he is honored as a *kami* (spirit) who protects the weak, maintains justice, and guards against fire. Hoin's grandfather was the famous samurai Katagiri Katsumoto (1556–1615), one of the Seven Spears of Shizugatake. Osumi's gifts as a healer and spiritual teacher were respected in Japan, and her clients included many renowned artists, national treasures, scientists, and leaders. Despite this recognition and her strong spiritual and cultural lineage, Osumi refused to accept offers to turn her work into a religion.

Two books have been written on Osumi's life—*The Shamanic Healer: The Healing World of Ikuko Osumi and the Traditional Art of Seiki Jutsu* (by Ikuko Osumi and Malcolm Ritchie) and *Ikuko Osumi, Sensei: Japanese Master of Seiki Jutsu* (by Bradford Keeney), and she is referred to as a Shinto shamaness by author George Williams in *Religions of the World: Shinto*. In this book we present how Osumi taught this natural way of healing and revitalization.

In 1996, Osumi Sensei passed her lineage to Bradford Keeney and legally authorized him to oversee its teaching. We will discuss the origin of The Keeney Institute for Healing, dedicated to passing on the basic principles and practices of seiki jutsu as a powerful means of transformation and personal development.

## BASIC IDEAS OF SEIKI JUTSU

The tradition of seiki jutsu holds that seiki is the vital force in nature and that it underlies all life and creation, from daily health to creative expression, actualization of human potential, and mastery of any form of performance art. Seiki jutsu practitioners propose that there is no need to seek an elaborate understanding of seiki, for any intellectual encapsulation brings unnecessary constraint. And more importantly, any presumed understanding of seiki may inhibit its evocation or felt presence.

Words such as *seiki* and *vital life force* are not limited to signifying physical energy and forces that belong to the laws of physics; they are also poetic metaphors that hint at the wholeness of life and how it can be experienced. Though seiki may be felt as an electrical force surging through the body, any reference to this experience as an "energy" or "force" is better taken as a holistic metaphor. In the same way that a person can poetically say that she has "fallen in love," been "struck by God," or "slain in the spirit," seiki is a way of indicating heightened ways of feeling alive.

Seiki is present in other cultural healing traditions. Osumi Sensei proposed that seiki has benefited people in every corner of the world, although it is called by many different names and is exercised in many different ways. This relationship to the unspeakable vitality of living is found in one of the world's oldest living cultures, the Kalahari Bushmen (or San), whose word *n/om* has a meaning similar to *seiki*. Bushmen regard the quality of their life as inseparable from their relationship to n/om, the dynamic underlying creation, change, and transformation. They will not utter the word whenever they are experiencing n/om, nor do they regard any exposition over the nature of its reality as relevant to having access to it.[2] Similarly, the tradition of seiki jutsu postulates that the word *seiki* only points to the vital life force, while explaining little about it.

Seiki is believed to be in all of nature—from the atmosphere to redwood forests, from English gardens to architectural spaces, in jazz, ballet, and human beings. Wherever there is creation and life, seiki is present.

Anyone alive has seiki, or to articulate it circularly, life is made alive by seiki. When seiki is depleted, a person becomes vulnerable to fatigue, apathy, and even illness. The key to well-being and revitalization lies in replenishing oneself with seiki. The same is true for effective action, such as artistic performance, scientific invention, therapeutic intervention, or spiritual practice. Without seiki, all spiritual, creative, therapeutic, and self-help approaches are severely limited.

Though having seiki may experientially feel analogous to filling a vehicle with fuel, there is more to seiki than the amount of life circulating inside a system. Seiki is also a way of tuning the whole organism, a process akin to tuning a musical instrument. If a string instrument is out of tune, no profound music can be created on it no matter how much skill the musician may have. The instrument must be tuned in order for a performance to reach and deliver its utmost expression. The same is true for human beings.

The primary idea of seiki jutsu is that spontaneous, automatic movement of the body is a natural means of holistic tuning, which in turn enables seiki to flow unimpeded. The result is that one feels full of seiki.

The practice of spontaneous movement is found in various therapeutic professions. For instance, hypnotherapists pay attention to ideomotor body responses, like a trembling finger or body twitch; these automatisms are believed to be conveyors of unconscious communication. Among movement therapists, spontaneous motor responses are used to help facilitate symptomatic release and trigger new forms of flexibility.

As a therapeutic application, what makes seiki jutsu unique is that it does not regard spontaneous movement as a technique serving a larger model or strategy of healing and transformation. With seiki jutsu, the movement is the whole process of change in and of itself. Automatic expression becomes the teacher, teaching, tuning, therapy, healing, spiritual practice, and goal all at once. Seiki jutsu emphasizes spontaneous performance that serves change. It is improvisational, interacting with all of the forces it encounters—including its own expression—to bring forth significant changes that inspire ever new expressions.

As a seiki jutsu practitioner learns to allow the performance of spontaneous, improvised movement to occur, she finds that the body awakens new repertoires of expression. What at first may be limited to rocking and other simple motions may later move into trembling hands, bouncing, a pumping abdomen, and swinging arms and continue into dance-like choreographies. This development and broadening of the possibilities of spontaneous performance mark the ways in which a practitioner's relationship to seiki grows. As the performance becomes more complex and unpredictable, so does the practitioner. In other words, as movement possibilities grow, the person's life grows as well, awakening more possibilities for bringing seiki-filled improvisational action into daily life, relationships, and profession.

Seiki jutsu teaches us how to access flow experience and be inside the moving stream of life. Here free movement also includes free speech, and the latter is regarded as another spontaneous performance of the whole body. There is no necessary mind-body dualism in this practice, as the production of ideas, thoughts, and speech require the body to produce and express them. Seiki jutsu brings forth more possibilities for voicing one's discourse, as well as relating to it in ways that are not attached to any particular narrative or preferred interpretation of lived experience.

The more seiki you have circulating inside you, the more likely your production of sound will distance itself from everyday speech and move toward ecstatic sound improvisation. Under the influence of seiki you lean toward becoming more metaphorical and poetic, and you may even

speak in rhyme—you'll see several places in this book where (seiki) h
urged us down this rhyming path.

## PREPARING THE CLIENT FOR SEIKI

Although seiki jutsu as a self-healing and revitalization practice can
be done without any professional assistance, it is initially helpful to
have a master performer of spontaneous movement get you on track
and in synch with these effortless motions.* The seiki jutsu master is
like a performing arts teacher whose job is to help others find their
own voice, movement, and way of participating inside creative expression. When a master of seiki jutsu spontaneously moves, a client can
be inspired to start his own motion. Or a client can hold on to the
hand or body of a master, whose natural movements can then be felt
in the client's body.

For example, the vibrating hand of a master can help activate the
same frequency of vibration in the client if the client is ready and
responsive to this transference of movement. Both seiki jutsu *senseis*
(master teachers) and Kalahari *n/om-kxaosi* (Bushman traditional healers) use their hands, arms, feet, legs, chests, and whole bodies to send
vibrations into the bodies of others. At first this is a means of helping jump-start an automatism in the client; later it enables rhythmic
entrainment, "going on a ride" with another more experienced practitioner of spontaneous movement. When the client's body allows the
vibrations to precipitate her own movements, both bodies can become
organized by one interactional vibration that orchestrates collaborative
movement. Here the movement rather than the person embodying it
is regarded as primary. The master practitioner has more experience

---

*A "master" of seiki jutsu is a respect term for someone who has mastered this art, in the
same way one would speak of a master artist, musician, or dancer. In seiki jutsu, however,
a master is a source of seiki in addition to being someone who can talk about it. Though
many have been practitioners of seiki jutsu, there have been only a few masters per generation in the tradition's known history.

"catching" the rhythm and movement and encourages the client to be carried into it through their interaction.

As the client becomes more familiar with spontaneous expression, there is less need for body contact, while paradoxically, more of this kind of interaction may naturally take place. A shift takes place where vibratory words, chants, and songs alone are sufficient to awaken automatisms and movement. Seiki jutsu refers to this stage of interaction as preparing someone to receive seiki. The Bushmen refer to this as helping make someone soft enough to receive an arrow of n/om. Each master practitioner has his or her own ways of emphasizing how to soften and make others ready for the reception of seiki. Keep in mind that the client already has seiki—anyone alive does, by definition—but the transmission of seiki (or the receiving of an arrow of n/om) refers to the readiness for a more intimate encounter with the vital life force and a greater capacity to express spontaneous movement.

In the transmission of seiki, also called "giving seiki," the client sits on a wooden seiki stool or bench while the master of seiki jutsu begins to awaken the seiki in the room; the master's task is to amplify, heat, and thicken that flowing current and direct it into the client's body. Classically, the seiki is awakened in the room by the practitioner making percussive drumming sounds, shouting, and whirling his arms over the client's head. To the practitioner, the air above the client can feel like a honey-like substance ready to be spread on the client's head. Traditionally, other people were not permitted to be in the room because it was believed that the strong currents of enhanced seiki can pull the life force out of their bodies, depleting and putting them at risk for illness.*

---

*We have not found this to be true in our experience, nor is this concern present in all healing cultures who have relationship to the non-subtle vital life force, including the Kalahari Bushmen, where n/om is typically shared with the whole community present. We find that emphasizing too much caution or taboo in relationship to seiki risks feeding unnecessary dualisms and explanations about it. For a strong n/om-kxao (Bushman doctor) or master of seiki jutsu, all wise discernment regarding the handling of seiki naturally arises to serve the particularities of the moment and is subject to change, without need for static rules.

As this frenzy of ecstatic expression hits a peak, the practitioner places his hands on the crown of the client's head. At this moment, enhanced seiki travels down the spine of the client. When it reaches the base of the spine, where it is believed to be stored, it typically triggers a swaying motion. The client is then congratulated and told that she has received seiki.

There are times when seiki is so amplified that a client's reception results in a startling, almost super-human performance of spontaneous movement. A professor in Japan, Dr. Burton Foreman, received seiki from Osumi Sensei and found himself propelled off the bench with his head touching the floor in front of him, only to be bounced all the way backward to touching the floor with his head in the other direction. Back and forth this went as if he were a gymnast performing what appeared to be prodigious movements. Here we see a similarity to complex *kriyas* known to some practitioners of kundalini yoga and familiar to Bushman n/om-kxaosi, among other ecstatic traditions.

The master of seiki jutsu eventually calms down the enhanced seiki and taps the base of the client's spine to still the motion, or at least slow it down. At this moment the client is given instruction in the use of her seiki stool or bench and the daily practice of seiki jutsu as a self-healing, self-revitalization, and self-teaching method.

## THE DAILY SEIKI EXERCISE

The daily exercise of seiki, traditionally called *seiki taisou,* helps maintain well-being and health, and contributes to opening access to the creative unconscious mind. Details for the daily exercise are outlined in chapter 4, "The Daily Seiki Exercise."

As a practitioner gains competency in hosting spontaneous body movement, the exercise becomes a time for releasing tiredness and for bringing seiki into the body. As Osumi Sensei described it, "Seiki taisou gives rhythm to your body similar to the way music conveys inspiration through vibration."[3] As the practice develops over the years, new kinds of movements will spontaneously arise. What is most important is not being attached to any particular form of movement other than spontaneity—that which happens effortlessly and naturally.

In 1920s Japan, a popular hygiene method known as Self-Improvement Life Force Therapy included seiki practice. It was thought that "seiki stimulates the exhausted nerves of the body and causes a reflex movement in the muscular system," referring to the automatic rocking motion that seiki inspires. Through this movement and the other spontaneous motions it triggers, seiki is known to instill health and help practitioners recover from illness, awaken a person's inborn talents, and open practitioners to dynamic spirituality.

The daily practice of the seiki exercise optimizes and nurtures the instilled seiki, making it available for self-healing and revitalization. However, Osumi Sensei believed it was not possible to master self-healing seiki therapy without the assistance of a seiki master. As she stated: "As priming water is necessary for pumping a well, so is the guidance and practice necessary for seiki jutsu."[4] Once transmitted, seiki is believed to stay with the human being for his or her entire lifetime.

The human body hosts a complex weave of many rhythms; balancing those many rhythms contributes to building a strong foundation for and maintaining good health. The natural movements that seiki evokes can be seen as helping bring the body's rhythms into a tuned alignment. Osumi Sensei proposed that a daily practice of seiki will help to dissipate the day's exhaustion and stress. In the beginning stages of seiki practice, the rocking motions will induce a natural kinetic trance that will refresh and stimulate. Later, the practitioner will find that her hands start to touch and pat her own body as if they are administering self-treatment. This is when natural healing takes place. The practitioner will do this spontaneously as if her hands have a mind of their own. It is not uncommon for seasoned practitioners to begin to voice energetic sounds, chants, or songs as this work takes place. All of this expression is regarded as a consequence of the unfolding of seiki teaching.

## USING SEIKI WITH OTHERS

As seiki is nurtured and deeply trusted in the daily practice, it will direct one's life in unexpected ways. As the seiki matures within a person, she may be naturally led to enter into healing movement interaction with others. Typically this starts with one's family members but may conceivably lead to becoming a member of the healing professions. Keep in mind, however, that the purpose of developing a relationship to seiki is not to become a healer or even necessarily a master of seiki jutsu, though that may occur. The latter are less a matter of will or conscious choice than they are something that naturally unfolds. Seiki jutsu does not value healing more than any other destiny or life path, and it will tune and revitalize your life and work and awaken your unique gifts whether you are a lawyer, musician, cook, parent, bartender, scientist, nurse, or factory worker.

*Purpose*

Seiki as a healing orientation has been called a "one-being therapy"[5] because it transcends the dichotomy between client and practitioner. Both receiver and transmitter of seiki are found inside their moving interaction. Seiki jutsu is applicable to both bodywork and therapeutic conversation. While Osumi Sensei brought seiki into bodywork, we have introduced seiki to therapeutic conversation,[6] the topic of chapter 6, "Seiki Conversation: The New Future of the Talking Cure." The talking cures of psychotherapy, counseling, and coaching have largely been absent of any awareness of whether they hold or promote the vital life force. While therapists argue over theoretical understandings and clinical methods, it is rare to hear anyone ask whether a clinical session has any vital life force. A seiki-charged conversation brings life to a session and is directed by interaction with a client's communications, both verbal and nonverbal. Like therapeutic bodywork, the therapist listens to the calling of the client to direct how to proceed.

A seiki-filled therapist, counselor, or life coach brings talk that inspires and fosters transformation of both client and practitioner. Here one does not know what she will say in a session until the moment she is inspired to talk. In addition to spontaneous talk, the manner of voicing words is also shaped by how the life force brings it forth. Free of attachment to therapeutic models, this practitioner is improvisational and ready to be moved by seiki. Seiki jutsu requires a mind that is ready to be filled and emptied as seiki calls it to act. This improvisational readiness has important implications for the movement-based arts, whether they regard themselves as therapeutic or not. Learning moves away from attachment to theoretical assumptions, sequences of choreography, and habits of performance and toward uninformed availability—the readiness for a surprise that can inspire performance. The movement from in-forming to per-forming, though perhaps better appreciated in dance, is less familiar to practitioners of therapy and healing. The latter professions are often entrenched in the replication of modeled procedures rather than improvisational performance. Seiki offers an empty-of-assumption availability, a readiness to dance with any emergent and passing form.

Some of the movement practices from Asia also suffer from pedagogies that first ask a student to memorize a form, practice it for years, and then hope that it will arise spontaneously in the future. The blind spot in this method is that it teaches non-spontaneity as a means to achieve spontaneity. The wisdom of seiki jutsu, Bushman healing, and other similar orientations is that they start at the end. In the beginning, the student and client are taught to be spontaneous. Though such an invitation invites paradox (being spontaneous in response to an invitation to purposefully perform it implies a self-referential contradiction), the masterful teacher and practitioner can arrange situations where free improvisation arises naturally.* This requires that a practitioner be spontaneous. And a client can, from time to time, allow herself to hold on to her teacher's spontaneity and be inspired by it to awaken her own uninformed performance of natural presence.

Seiki opens the door to the mysteries of spirituality, healing, and well-being. The healers of one of the oldest living cultures in the world, the

---

*Teacher: "Be spontaneous!"
Student: "I can't because I'd only be doing what you told me to purposefully perform."
Teacher: "Never mind that! Be spontaneous!"

Kalahari Bushmen (or the San), have a strong relationship to this vital life energy. In fact, the Bushmen arguably could be regarded as the first masters of seiki jutsu. The Bushmen have long known that this non-subtle life force can awaken the most extraordinary experiences possible for a human being, what we call "the original mysteries."

Over several decades Brad became recognized as one of the strongest healers, or n/om-kxaosi, among the Bushmen in southern Africa. He not only became deeply involved with the Bushmen as a healer, he befriended and conducted research with most of the elder men and women n/om-kxaosi across Botswana and Namibia (see Bradford Keeney, *Ropes to God, Kalahari Bushman Healers, Bushman Shaman,* and *The Bushman Way of Tracking God*). Brad's groundbreaking research on the Bushmen's healing ways is honored at the Origins Centre, a world heritage museum in Johannesburg, South Africa. A mentorship in seiki jutsu necessarily includes what the Bushmen teach about the non-subtle life force and the amazing ways its mysteries are able to transform your life.

*Symptoms*

Whenever very strong seiki flows within you, it is natural for it to be accompanied by trembling, shaking, quaking, and an experience of ecstatic bliss. This transformative experience is an entry into numinous spirituality—the awesome presence of divinity that inspires you to tremble in awe as the source of life's vitality surges through you. All religions and pre-religions initially recognized this ecstasy and regarded the *mysterium tremendum et fascinans* as the source of what can heal, transform, and revitalize. A direct contact experience with God or holiness will leave you unable to sit still and be quiet. It is so overwhelmingly thrilling and exhilarating that you can't help but sing and dance. We hope that this book will give you the tools and the inspiration to make a visit every day to your own Life Force Theatre, where through your practice of seiki jutsu you will gain access to the flow of life force energy inside you and discover the joy of a life "performed" by seiki.

# 2

# IKUKO OSUMI SENSEI AND THE LINEAGE OF SEIKI JUTSU

In ancient Japan a timeless treasure was kept alive. Even under difficult times of conflict and war, samurai warriors safeguarded its presence. Sometimes it went underground and was kept secret. In the last century, a remarkable woman—we often call her our samurai grandmother—was the last member of old Japan to be its custodian. This treasure, seiki jutsu, is now in our hands, and we pass it on to you.

Inside the seiki dreaming we see Ikuko Osumi Sensei waving her hands at the sky. She is making loud noises with the release of intensified seiki. Both earth and sky awaken as birds begin to circle and animals gather round to pay homage to the circulating life. Her arm is now straight as her fingers point at a gathering of trees. She shouts—"Vvvooot!"—and seiki is propelled outward. Fruit suddenly blossoms on the tree limbs—miraculously, each tree carries the fruit of the world. Apples, pears, bananas, mangoes, papayas, and all the other fruits fall gently from the tree, landing softly on the ground. They roll toward her, making a feast for those who hunger for vital living.

Osumi Sensei chooses an apple and a lemon and makes a juice out of them. "Here, drink this every day for the rest of your life. It will help you breathe seiki. Do so in order to live fully and become the destiny that is calling you." You reach out for the glass of juice and notice that it has turned to a luminous white fog. You drink it. The glass is full of seiki. It travels down your body, warming everything inside. You begin to tremble, for it is bringing new life to your body.

*Daily Juice!*

"Drink seiki," she announces. "Only seiki can quench the thirst you seek to satisfy. Do not be deceived by the lost meandering of mind. Drink the stream that returns you to the source. You cannot bear fruit without it."

The vital life force speaks inside this dreaming, for its voice is not separate from our own. Osumi Sensei is its ambassador, as are all who enter the stream and drink it. We hear someone say, "Stop searching for the right answer, the best philosophy, the truest spirituality. They are nothing without seiki. With seiki, they deliver the same truth."

We introduce you to a Japanese master whose life story is a glass of seiki. Drink, and bring forth the fruit you are meant to deliver.

---

Ikuko Osumi Sensei was one of the greatest healers and masters of the vital life force during the twentieth century, yet neither she nor the tradition of seiki jutsu are well known today. This is testimony to its formerly hidden and often secret history. It is also likely a consequence of how far today's healing practices have drifted from their original sources and forms. This Japanese tradition of self-healing and revitalization is known to have existed in the early times of Shintoism, perhaps as far back as the eighth century.

Practiced as a daily rejuvenation ritual by the samurai, seiki jutsu was well established centuries before reiki was developed. It carries ancient Japanese shamanic ways of ecstatically handling the non-subtle life force. Today's only remaining lineage of seiki jutsu teaching was held and passed on by Ikuko Osumi Sensei, of Setagaya, Tokyo, Japan, to Bradford Keeney. Over all these centuries it has remained in its original traditional form, without exploitation or commodification. We will provide a historical look at Osumi Sensei and her lineage, leading up to the emergence of seiki jutsu in our contemporary times.

Ikuko Osumi Sensei was a member of an old samurai family. As a child, Osumi Sensei was known to be spiritually gifted and powerfully clairvoyant. People came to her to find out about their illness, to ask if they would have a baby, and for other advice regarding important life decisions. As a youngster she could even predict when someone would die and see how it would happen. Having an uncanny ability to predict the weather, she would climb the local mountain every morning to wave red or white flags to indicate to the fishermen what weather they could expect before they went out to sea, signaling them whether it would be a clear day or if they should prepare for a storm. She was loved by all the villagers.

Osumi Sensei's grandfather, Katagiri, was a wealthy and influential man in the northeastern region of Japan. After a tragic tsunami nearly destroyed the entire area where they lived, her grandfather spent the family fortune helping rebuild the city and constructed a massive breakwater project in Shiogama so that life, property, and fishing boats would be protected in the future. Katagiri was following in the footsteps of his ancestors—Osumi Sensei's family was already known for the sacrifices they had made to help people. Her ancestor Eizon Hoin, a Buddhist priest who lived in the 1600s, became known for numerous miracles and is honored today as a kami (spirit) who protects the weak, maintains justice, and guards against fire. Hoin's grandfather was the famous samurai

Katagiri Katsumoto (1556–1615), one of the Seven Spears of Shizugatake.

In 1641, Eizon Hoin was appointed to restore the shrine on the sacred mountain of Makiyama, which had been established seventeen hundred years earlier. There he began his career as a spiritual teacher. When the Kitagami River became impassable for ships due to an accumulation of muddy silt, the local economy was threatened. After all human efforts to clear the channel failed, Hoin was asked to spiritually intervene. He prayed for three nights and four days at the shrine altar; at the end of the fourth day, a huge storm rolled in and caused extensive flooding that cleared the entire mouth of the river. Even the largest ships were now able to enter. The clan lord honored Hoin by giving him some land, but the local lord was jealous of the respected Buddhist priest. He intercepted the news and stole the land without Hoin ever knowing it had been meant for him.

Hoin continued to receive the devotion of the local people, and this made the lord even more jealous. He falsely accused Hoin of misdemeanors to hide his own crimes, but the people refused to believe that Hoin was guilty. The lord was relentless—finally the people were so filled with fear that they stopped going to the shrine to see Hoin. Only one man continued visting him; Hoin, in turn, expressed his gratitude by secretly making that man a talisman of protection to place in his house. Later, when the whole village was destroyed by fire, only that man's house remained untouched.

The lord was finally successful in accusing Hoin of false crimes. Hoin was sentenced to a lifetime of exile on a remote island. After praying night and day for several years, he announced that he would die. He then stared at the sky and died without a single tear. His final request to be buried upside down was not fulfilled, and immediately a disease and fever fell upon all the people. Worse, no one could catch a single fish, which was a disaster for a fishing community. The people finally dug up Hoin's body and turned him upside down. In short order, everything returned to normal.

Like his samurai ancestor, Katagiri Katsumoto, Hoin became

known historically as an upholder of justice who himself was a victim of tragedy. Katagiri became more of a court samurai than a warrior, but he too found himself living in the midst of a ruthless leader. His anguish was later dramatized in Kabuki theatre, where Katsumoto is depicted as a tragic figure, not unlike Hamlet. In Tsubouchi Shoyo's play *Kiri-hitoha*, Katsumoto is the main character, a good man caught helpless in the chaos of dynastic struggle. The play, published in 1894–95 and first staged in 1904, is widely regarded as the best modern Kabuki piece written by one of the most celebrated playwrights of modern Japan and made Katagiri Katsumoto a household name. *Kiri-hitoha* remains one of the most popular and highly regarded modern Kabuki plays.

Katsumoto died only twenty days after the fall of the Osaka castle, presumably through *seppuku* (samurai ritual suicide).

Osumi grew up knowing about these ancestors. Each had fought for justice, become a historical figure in Japanese history, and suffered greatly with a tragic death. Her own life was also filled with pain and suffering. As she once told Brad, "I have always thought that difficulty or hardship was my way." She believed this was true for all spiritual healers and teachers.

Throughout her life, she dreamed of the tidal wave that took place before she was born, destroying her grandfather's village.

I have been haunted by the story my grandfather told me about a great tidal wave. It touched my dreams. I experienced the roar of the Sanriku tidal wave, a devastating event that occurred before I was born. I still dream of it today. My grandfather, who owned the local fishing fleet and several large rice fields, told me how my grandmother and aunt had crouched in the corner of the twelve-mat room on the second floor of his immense home. He watched them bow again and again toward the sea, praying to every Shinto god and Buddhist saint for deliverance. The fearsome tidal wave that Grandfather had predicted would strike our coast was bearing down upon them. "This is exactly why I had a two-story house built!" my grandfather shouted out. In my imagination I could see his silhouette against the night sky, straight and firm. "It's a gigantic crest moving toward us!" my grandfather soon proclaimed. And as my aunt tells the story, he didn't move a centimeter away from the window. She admired his courage. He stood leaning forward and peering unafraid at the roaring sea as it advanced toward him, creeping right up to the foundation of his house. He watched stoically as the sea swirled around and carried almost everything back to sea with it—houses, trees, and people. The village was destroyed in front of his eyes.

While her grandfather rebuilt the village of Gamo, he never recouped the money and lost his entire fortune. He aged quickly and soon died. The vision of her grandfather witnessing the death of all those fishermen inspired Osumi toward the goal of becoming a doctor who could help people with their suffering. Her father was very ill when she was a child, and he died when he was only thirty-six from a "sickness of the lungs." His death also strengthened Osumi's desire to become a healer. Before he died, she held his hand and promised that she would grow up to become a healer so she could help him. Her father's last words to her were, "Go to Tokyo, Ikuko, and be of service to the villagers."

When she was fifteen years old, Osumi Sensei moved in with her mother's brother in Tokyo. Instead of sending her to medical school, her uncle had traditional Japanese arts taught to her, such as tea ceremony, calligraphy, and flower arranging. Osumi Sensei knew that her uncle and aunt were preparing her for a future marriage, and she was emotionally devastated. She became very sick and disillusioned.

She remembered that when she was a young girl, her family would visit the Makiyama Shrine on top of Maki Mountain, where her ancestor Eizon Hoin was honored. Her family and friends knew the legend of a white snake that lived in the shrine, which they believed protected them. Though no one had ever actually seen the snake, its cast-off skin was collected each year and used by her grandmother to make a medicine for treating wounds and warts. When Osumi Sensei was five years old, a ball that she was playing with rolled into the shrine. When she went to retrieve the ball the white snake presented itself, raised its head, and spoke to her: "I have fulfilled my duty and am tired. Over the years I have helped, healed, and protected many people, including your family. It is time for you to take over and carry on this work. You must do it now." The snake, the messenger of Eizon Hoin, then jumped into the left side of Osumi's physical body to live there as her guardian spirit helper.

*In the seiki dreamtime, the white guardian snake speaks for Hoin: "Throughout religion, mythology, and literature, I am a messenger for the vital life force, the source of creation. As I shed my skin, I invite rebirth, renewal, healing, transformation, and immortality. I guard certain sacred places and temples and holy messengers, entering into them to protect the temple of holy wisdom that they carry. When I swallow my tail and become a spinning Ouroboros, know that this circular motion points to the All-in-All, the infinite circularity of the self-creating universe. When I wrap myself around the Tree of Life, I become the axis of the world. Coiled inside of you, I am the vessel holding the flow of seiki." And then the ancestral guardian was silent.*

Ten years later, as her uncle prepared her for marriage, Osumi felt her life was drifting from her destiny of becoming a healer. As she fell into a self-described terrible, thick, black cloud, her uncle took her to many doctors, including Western and Chinese specialists. She did not improve and fell deeper into despair. Osumi became curious, however, about a daily practice her aunt was conducting. Every day her aunt, Mrs. Hayashibe, would go upstairs dressed in full kimono regalia and disappear into a small, three-mat room. Ikuko wondered what her aunt did in that small room. Finally, after many months of observing this routine, her aunt called her into the room. The year was 1935. What Mrs. Hayashibe said changed the course of Osumi's life.

Her aunt explained that every day at three o'clock she went into the three-mat room and conducted "seiki exercises." Her aunt told her: "I can't explain seiki to you, but I believe that seiki is the only thing left to cure you. I am sure I can cure you with it. Are you willing to try?" Without understanding what seiki was, Ikuko Osumi accepted her aunt's invitation. Her aunt then announced that she would "instill" seiki into her the very next afternoon.

Her aunt asked Ikuko to sit on a stool in the "seiki room," as her aunt called it. Ikuko Osumi knew her aunt was standing behind her but did not know what she was doing. She heard wild noises, unrecognizable sounds, and a lot of commotion. The only other thing she remembered about that afternoon was that she suddenly found herself moving around in a spontaneous way, rocking back and forth without any effort. It was as if some invisible force had entered her, causing her to move in this automatic motion. She had received seiki.

*The white snake spoke again: "I have been coiled inside you, ready for release, and waiting to climb. With these movements, feel that I am alive and carrying seiki to every part of you. Know in the deepest part of you that I am you, the luminosity that brings the light of visionary sight, enabling entry to the deepest oceans of wisdom and the heights of mystical flight." Then it was time to return and the snake fell silent.*

Her aunt proclaimed to Ikuko that maybe someday she would teach seiki, but then quickly warned, "Under no circumstances are you to teach any kind of seiki therapy. It's too dangerous." Ikuko noticed that her aunt's arms had turned purple; her aunt had to rest in bed for several days after this seiki installation to regain her energy. Although Ikuko's body knew how to move and rock on its own, she still didn't understand the mysterious force her aunt had given her.

A day or two after receiving seiki, her aunt instructed Ikuko about sitting on the seiki stool at least once a day for twenty minutes. She taught Ikuko to put the tips of her fingers together, press her closed eyes, and then wait and see what takes place. When Ikuko first did this, nothing happened. Then suddenly she began moving in a circular fashion and knew instantly that the seiki inside her was alive and causing her body to move in this self-propelled way.

Over the days, weeks, and months of her daily practice, she began feeling stronger and regaining her vitality. She eventually found that her hands became like dowsing rods or magnets, drawn to other parts of her body where she would apply therapeutic touch, the force of seiki carrying her hands to the places where healing was needed.

As she watched her body teach itself how to heal, Ikuko realized that she was going to grow up to become a different kind of doctor. She would help her family and others become well through the use of seiki. With seiki, Ikuko Osumi found the purpose of her life.

Seiki not only revealed a "strange, indefinable energy" that permeated her whole being; it both initiated a stirring within her and started an outer movement of her body. It enabled her to cure herself, and it opened the door to spiritual wisdom. Ikuko Osumi found that during her practice she could lose contact with the everyday world and "enter another dimension of the universe." She learned how to travel inside her own body and observe its inner workings. She entered into conversations with nature and learned about the interrelationship between the body and nature, which is the context of natural health. In this spiritual universe, she was taught how to be a great seiki healer and teacher.

*This is how it is when you ride the movements of the holy white snake. It takes you anywhere and everywhere, opening new eyes,*

*ears, and ways of sensing not known before. Enter the teaching of the moving light, its luminous absorption ready to seep inside of you. The river, when seen from the eagle's view, looks like a serpent glistening in the sun. This moving current waves its hands at sky and earth. Did you know that the etymology of the word wave means "to move back and forth?" Move. Back and forth is the motion, the creation of wave, the pulse of seiki.*

During the time with her aunt, Osumi wondered how she could ever give seiki to someone else. When her energy increased, her aunt offered the pathway to the next level of instruction: "As long as you expect to be taught how to instill seiki into others, rather than finding out for yourself, the more likely it is that you will never succeed. You must master it by yourself." Her aunt was teaching Ikuko that everything about seiki is natural, non-purposeful, and automatic. As the body moves on its own, teaching also spontaneously presents itself—effortlessly and naturally—when it is ready. The teaching cannot be willed or forced. It happens in its own way, under its own terms.

Ikuko Osumi realized there was no way to rationally figure out anything about seiki. It didn't help to think about it or wonder what should be done with it. She had only the deep recognition that the whole universe was somehow contained within her own body, that her body was a tiny universe of its own. She stopped trying to figure out anything about seiki and instead allowed the internal wisdom triggered by seiki to develop on its own.

*To seek seiki with the thinking mind is futile. You cannot figure anything out. What spiritual practice should I follow? What foods are the most healthy? How should I move forward with my relationship? What career is best for me? How can I find peace*

*and freedom from stress? How can I be healed? What is the secret to prosperity? How can I help save the world? You cannot think your way through life. Instead, let the radiance shine through and guide each step without your knowing the whole course that is emerging. Let seiki illumine and direct. Only then can your life grow in unexpected and delightful ways.*

Live

One day Ikuko Osumi's cousin arrived at the house very sick. Her aunt asked her cousin if he wanted to get well. "Of course I do," he replied. After a pause, Osumi's aunt said, "Then let us instill seiki into you." When Osumi heard the word *us* she was startled, wondering how she would be able to help her aunt instill seiki. Then, without warning, her aunt said, "Ikuko will instill seiki into you." The certainty in her aunt's voice filled Ikuko Osumi with a sudden surge of confidence that it was time for her to give seiki. At that moment she knew she was ready.

*If there is seiki, knowing is irrelevant. Feel this to be deeply true. Feel whatever is true and honor the truth of the feeling. A well-fed truth will grow and bring you along with it. Its movement, unfolding, and growth carries seiki.*

Ikuko Osumi had learned from her daily practice that everything associated with seiki happened on its own and did not require previous instruction. She believed that when it was time to instill it into her cousin, it would simply happen on its own. There was nothing to plan for or think about. She simply had to devote herself to being available for the seiki to work through her.

After several days, she led her cousin to the three-mat room without saying a word. She sat him on the stool and stood behind him, as her aunt had done with her. Then the seiki took over. Her hands began moving in the air with great force; instantly Osumi knew that the essence of transmission was in the hands and fingers. Her hands quickly moved over her cousin's head, looking as if they were groping toward something invisible to others.

That was when her arms started to periodically bang against the wall. The sound of the impact sent a strange resonance into her head, and that was when she realized that this kind of sound was necessary for transmission. Spontaneously, she began taking in deep breaths of air and blowing them out with great force as she hit the walls with the palms of her hands. All the noises she was making triggered vibrations in her body. As she described it, "the room was electrified with sound, vibration, and movement."

At the peak of this ecstatic frenzy, with trembling fingers and a shaking body, Ikuko Osumi suddenly let her hands be dramatically grabbed and pulled to the top of her cousin's head, as if a magnet was drawing them there. The force of the movement shocked her. Then something took place that she was not prepared for. Within a second or two, she felt "a bolt of electricity move through my hands into my cousin's head. I knew this was seiki."

*The white serpent messenger of Hoin is standing straight up, like a bolt of lightning shot from a stormy sky. The white lightning speaks with thundering authority: "If you haven't made these sounds, felt this resonance, experienced this motion, emotion, and commotion, then you have not come face to face with seiki. You are still sleeping, perhaps dreaming that you are awake. Wake up! Surrender to the truth of what you are. Let this truth strike you like lightning!"*

When the bolt came through her hands, her cousin's head slipped away from her and he began to move in back-and-forth motions. Ikuko was delirious with excitement. She had instilled seiki for the first time. As her cousin rocked back and forth, she felt as though she were walking on a cloud. Her aunt entered the room and proclaimed with a big smile, "That, Ikuko, is seiki. You have mastered it at last." Suddenly Osumi felt bewildered, realizing she had been taught nothing other than confidence in seiki. Later she would come to realize that by seeking more knowledge and systematic teaching about seiki, she was "searching for the point of the arrow instead of sharpening it myself." Her aunt had been a great teacher—she had taught Ikuko Osumi to learn only from seiki.

Near the end of the war Osumi Sensei moved deep inside the country, where hard physical labor overwhelmed and exhausted her. She was working so hard that she forgot about her seiki practice. When her ill health reached the breaking point, Osumi began her seiki practice again. Her health returned as seiki began to permeate her body. At first it didn't cause any physical movement, but the inner stirring she had felt when she first received seiki returned and grew until she started spontaneously moving again. As she said: "For the second time in my life, seiki saved me, and I again discovered I had the means for curing myself." The daily practice of seiki throws off exhaustion and brings a surge of new energy. For Osumi Sensei, seiki is the key to health and well being.

*Even a master wakes up each morning knowing nothing and must be created all over again. Do not forget that you must always be reborn. Each day seiki must renew and rebirth your presence in the stream of life. Move in order to move again. Be spontaneous as a means of spontaneously being alive.*

Years later Brad would climb those same stairs, enter the three-mat room, sit on the seiki bench, and feel the force of seiki come into his body. Months after he first heard about Ikuko Osumi, Brad was contacted by Dr. Kenji Kameguchi, professor of clinical psychology at the University of Tokyo, asking him to deliver a keynote address at the tenth anniversary gathering of the Japanese Association of Family Psychology. Brad accepted the invitation and quickly asked if they could help him locate Ikuko Osumi Sensei. Brad mentioned that one of her patients had been Dr. Takehi Hashimoto, a professor of anatomy at Toho University Medical School, and that he had written the foreword to one of Ikuko Osumi's books.

After trying to find him, Professor Kameguchi wrote that Dr. Hashimoto had recently passed away and that he had no other way to find out where Osumi lived. Several months passed. The night before Brad was to depart for Tokyo, he received a fax from his host saying he was delighted to announce that he had found Osumi Sensei. She lived very close to the auditorium at Showa Women's University in Setagaya, Tokyo, the place where Brad was scheduled to give his speech. Osumi Sensei had been contacted and was eager to meet Brad.

After Brad gave his speech in 1992, he was taken to Osumi's home. She greeted him in a traditional kimono made of eggshell-white satin, with a single-lined, angular design of sand-colored trees with entwined branches. The first thing Osumi Sensei did was stare into Brad's eyes and begin to recount his entire life history, including detailed information about his grandfather, father, and son. Brad was so shocked he didn't know whether to shout, cry, or faint. Then she surprised him further by saying, "You must cancel your trip home and live with me. I will teach you how to make everything you know become one."

Brad knew he couldn't refuse her invitation. The truth surrounding its delivery and the rock-solid authority of her presence could not be ignored. Then he became a bit worried, remembering the stories about others who had tried to learn from her. In order to become a *deshi*, or apprentice to Osumi Sensei, it was necessary to sacrifice oneself. The sensei-deshi (master-apprentice) relationship was brutal, and to some Western eyes could be excessive and cruel. A professor from Europe had come to Osumi and was instructed to clean her floors for several years. The professor had a nervous breakdown under this teaching relationship.

To Brad's surprise, however, he was not ordered to clean floors or perform the typical tasks of a deshi. Instead, Osumi gave Brad a place in her home that was the equivalent to that of a son. He was watched over and nurtured by her caring supervision. However, Osumi Sensei held nothing back in the offering of her teaching and guidance. She was forthright and direct in her teaching, and the brutal truths she revealed to Brad were sometimes startling. Over time Brad was introduced to many of her esteemed patients and entered the homes of some of Japan's national treasures. Brad watched how she worked with people and how she gave seiki.

Sometimes Brad would test Sensei. For example, during a weekend trip to Kyoto he thought to himself, "Though I enjoy Japanese food, what I really desire most right now is some fried chicken." During the train ride back to Tokyo, he included another food desire: "Let's add some vanilla ice cream to that order." He chuckled to himself and wondered what Sensei would think if she could read his mind. When Brad arrived back at her home, Osumi and her cook were waiting for him with smiles, holding a large plate of fried chicken. A gigantic bowl of vanilla ice cream followed for dessert.

One of Brad's interpreters, Dr. Burton Foreman, a professor of English at a university in Tokyo, told a remarkable story about what had happened to him with Osumi. He had started experiencing a kind of paralysis; after finding that no doctor could help him, he called Osumi Sensei. Before he could fully explain the situation to her, she immediately told him what had happened. Then she went on to tell Dr. Foreman the cause of his condition. He had recently dug up a place in his backyard to build a fish pond; while digging, he broke a buried ceramic pot. Osumi instructed him: "The pot you broke was a burial urn. I will give you some salt and sake for you to sprinkle over that area. Each day for a week, you must go to your garden and smile at the place where the urn used to reside." Dr. Foreman followed her instructions, and his physical problem quickly disappeared.

Dr. Foreman was later given seiki by Osumi Sensei on July 4, 1976. He became the first non-Japanese person to receive its transmission. He describes what took place:

What happened was a very strange and wholly unexpected experience for me. On that day I was seated on a stool in a small room. With Osumi were two assistants. They all stood behind me. I waited patiently, although apprehensively. The time had arrived for me to receive seiki. I felt nervous. Quite suddenly and entirely unexpectedly, there arose behind me the most dreadful din I have ever heard in my life. I heard shouting, hissing, and then the sound of pounding. I realized all three of them were hitting the *fusuma* [sliding doors] with the open palms of their hands.

I experienced another shock when one of the assistants began to breathe into my right ear in an ever-increasing crescendo until he was hissing, blowing out puffs of air, and uttering meaningless bursts of sound, while the other two were shouting at the top of their lungs, giving forth meaningless yells and shrieks, which produced in total the most God-awful racket one could ever imagine.

I sat there shocked. I shall never forget that moment when, quite suddenly, I felt something come down from above me, from the direction of the ceiling, down above my head. Something was entering my head in the back where the hair-whorl is located.

I thought: "My God! This is it!" It was like an electric shock, yet it moved slowly down the back of my neck and into my spinal column. I felt frightened for the first time. Whatever it was, it was inside me and moving down my back. I can say this about it: it was something with a purpose.

But then what followed was even more surprising and unexpected. I saw Osumi and her two disciples appear at my right side looking at me expectantly. The moving sensation in my body reached the very bottom limits of my spinal cord—the tailbone—and I knew that that was its destination. I was then suddenly thrown forward on my stool in a violent thrust surging up from my tailbone. The upward surge threw me completely off the stool.

The surprise of it staggered me. But one of the disciples shouted at me: "Get back on the stool!" I scrambled back up, but hardly had I sat down again when, just as unexpectedly, I was next drawn back in a swift pull from behind and jerked so far that my legs flew up in the air directly over my head. I can remember the surprise of that so well, because I did not fall over backward off the stool as I most certainly would have under ordinary conditions. Before I could fully digest this very strange situation, I was again pulled forward in a violent thrust from my hips. My legs slammed down on the floor and my face all but banged into them. Then I was pulled backward again. My feet were high up in the air again and I was tottering on the edge of the stool. I felt entirely secure in whatever had gripped me in its most powerful, vise-like control . . .

"Congratulations!" Osumi cried to me, finally. "You have received seiki. It is with you for life. Cherish it."

Like everyone else who had been there before, when Brad entered Osumi Sensei's room to receive seiki he heard the noises, the banging, the hissing, and the shouting prior to her hands coming down on the crown of his head. He felt his body being rocked and shaken, vibrating internally and externally. Brad recognized what had been familiar to him ever since having a similar experience when he was a university undergraduate student. Unlike her other clients, with Brad Osumi Sensei found a friend and colleague who was already full of seiki and was intimately familiar with the vital life force.

*The white serpent sings again: We are old friends, older than time itself. I live inside both of you and your meeting helps bring you more together as one. Each of you has a mission and that includes your sharing together what each has been given. Why Brad? Why Ikuko? Nothing about this can be explained. It is simply seiki. The ocean of seiki holds everyone, as any ocean contains every drop of water inside it. Inside of Brad is an awakened wave, the same one that speaks inside of Ikuko. A new son for an ancient mother gives light to what is rarely seen. Let the ancestral sun shine and rebirth the primal mother! So is the way of Ouroboros, the spinning back and forth that changes everything—making the first the last and the last the first, creating new beginnings for old endings as new futures emerge from old histories. Enter into the circulation of the ever-turning circle of life.*

Over the years Osumi Sensei tried to share everything she had experienced with Brad, preparing him to teach about it to others. When he was funded for over a decade to study healing traditions around the world, he would tell her what he had learned about seiki in other traditions. Once he showed her a film of the Kalahari Bushmen healing dance, and she became very excited, pointing at the screen and shouting, "Seiki! Seiki!" She recognized and celebrated Brad's reports on seiki, the mysterious, indescribable force that causes the body to spontaneously move and tremble, bringing about healing, well-being, and transformation. When she opened her personal vault and showed Brad a copy of a historical document written in 1928 by Jozo Ishii, he realized that Japan had been using the same ancient healing practice found in other parts of the world, including one of the world's oldest living cultures, the Bushmen (the San) of southern Africa.

Osumi explained how seiki jutsu was practiced privately in its early days and had been kept secret in Japan. It had supposedly been a part of the natural daily regime of the samurai warriors; each day they allowed their bodies to be moved by seiki. During the first years of the Sowa era, in the second half of the 1920s, a popular health movement called "self-improvement life force therapy" arose in Japan. Thousands of Japanese people had been moved into health by the natural movements of seiki jutsu. However, with the many changes that later swept through Japan, seiki jutsu all but disappeared from the country. It was kept alive, in an underground kind of way, through the hidden teaching practice of Osumi Sensei.

What makes seiki jutsu unique is its dedication to natural, automatic, spontaneous expression, rather than adherence to memorized forms. Osumi once told Brad, "Forget what you've been told about qigong, t'ai chi exercises, or any of the other Asian disciplines. Do not attempt preconceived forms or choreographed sequences of motions with names like 'grasping the bird's tail' or 'wave hands like clouds.' In this approach, which I feel is more natural, I want you to become empty and available. Wait for seiki to move you."

*Several old qigong masters survived their exile in the mountains of China, then came down and shared the wisdom of their form-less ways with a few. Like seiki jutsu and the Kalahari healing dance, their ways of practice were spontaneous. Their spontaneity was the teaching that awakened freedom from lifeless form, paving the way for perfect formless form, the movement back and forth, the interpenetration of emptiness and fullness, the dance of life and death, the marriage of sacred and profane, and all that is becoming as it is undone. Recognize the accidents that point to the natural way.*

There are times when people might see a seiki practitioner execute a perfect choreography that is recognizable and known, but when performed through seiki jutsu it happens without aim or purpose. The form spontaneously presents itself and then moves on to another movement. This is how all choreographed practices were originally invented—in a moment of non-purposeful perfection the mover was naturally and effortlessly moved, and then afterward the form was named and taught to others.

In this manner of teaching, things get turned upside down. The form is first demonstrated so the student can memorize and perfect it, and then the student hopes that someday, after years of practice, the form will manifest itself automatically, without any effort. Seiki jutsu, on the other hand, cultivates spontaneity and allows the art of improvisational movement to develop in its own way. This practice is regarded as a way of "milking the life force," bringing it into the body and circulating it through pulsing movements. Seiki jutsu reminds us that it is natural spontaneity, rather than any particular form, that is most important. It doesn't matter whether a movement is small or large or choreographed in any preferred way—it is natural and effortless expression that is most valued.

Not only the fingers, hands, arms, legs, and torso can move, but also the vocal cords. They are part of the body as well. All kinds of sounds may come forth when seiki is moving through you. These include hissing sounds and the exclamation of "Hai!" or "Vvvvooot!" A master of seiki is able to transmit and infuse seiki with spoken words and sounds. As we will later see, conversation charged with seiki transforms talk therapy into a more vibrant context for healing, giving it the life necessary to help change and transform others.

*"Yes, I did ask to be buried upside down," we hear Eizon Hoin say. "My truth is contrary to what others teach. I said then and I shout it out today: Talk is nothing unless it is voiced with seiki, the*

*vital life force." You must be ordained, anointed, and baptized in this holy vital life force. Otherwise, you are a messenger of death. Most therapy, as taught in the universities, professional training programs, and workshops, is a teaching of how not to be alive. The touch of therapy too often brings death, a cessation of the spontaneous flow of creative expression. Infuse therapy, healing, and spiritual practice with seiki or else face the fact that you are burying the truth upside down. The ancestors are watching, seeing what is actively true and what is lying down asleep.*

Osumi Sensei watched Brad give seiki to others. He found, in the same way she had with her aunt, that his hands and arms moved automatically as wild sounds emerged, bringing forth a sense of highly charged energy. When he placed his hands on a person's head, a bolt of energy went through him, transferring an energetic vibration to the person's body. The person would then rock, vibrate, shake, or feel ecstatic bliss. Osumi Sensei watched Brad give seiki to her daughter, Masako Hayashibe, who rocked, trembled, shook, and collapsed to the ground as she entered a deep kinetic trance. Osumi shouted, "Congratulations! That is strong seiki!"

*There is no giving seiki to another without giving seiki to yourself at the same time. Masako and I hold hands and feel like we have stepped into an ocean of energy that carries us somewhere else. Waves of energy pass through us as we jointly feel tingling sensations throughout our bodies. Then a lightning bolt of concentrated seiki gives us a sudden jolt. There is no need to comprehend or explain what takes place. It is a reality that does not require belief. It simply is what it is—an infusion of extraordinary exhilaration and energy. We are experiencing it and the*

*only words that can arise in our mind are those that can express gratitude. We can barely hold on as we fall into the current, fully immersed in its replenishing source. We are both energized, healed, tuned, and then brought back home. Strong seiki is shared seiki. "Congratulations, Masako. You have received seiki. Congratulations, we have received seiki today."*

Osumi Sensei flew to Brad's house in the United States and asked him to help her pour seiki into his son, Scott, who was a child at the time. When he placed his hands over his son's head next to hers, Brad felt a honey-like substance extending from the ceiling to the crown of his head. With Osumi and her assistant, Takafumi Okajima, they grabbed the pulsing, invisible, honey-like seiki, wiped it on Scott's head, then found their hands spontaneously clamped to the crown of his head. Scott immediately began to rock back and forth as his body was filled with seiki.

*Seiki can be experienced in many ways. Make sure you do not get attached to any conception about seiki. It is always changing. Whatever you think you know about seiki can interfere with its changing presence. Let seiki be what it needs to be. Do not let any pre-formed knowing make you blind to its next appearance.*

There is a Hollywood ending to Scott's encounter with seiki. The next day he played his last Little League game of the season. Osumi Sensei's Japanese delegation came to his game, which was held at a field in St. Paul, Minnesota. As always, Osumi Sensei arrived in her traditional attire. She and her colleagues patiently watched the entire game, clapping for Scott every time he did anything—when he stood up they clapped, and they clapped when he sat down. Whether on or off the field, their eyes were glued to him and they seemed to cheer for every breath and movement he made.

The score was tied going into the final inning. Scott went to bat with the bases loaded and worked himself into the classic bottom-of-the-last-inning situation: three balls and two strikes with two outs already chalked up. We can still hardly believe what happened. With the cracking sound of the hardball making perfect contact with his bat, Scott hit his first and only home run. The ball flew over the left-field fence; Scott had hit a grand slam to win the game. Ikuko Osumi Sensei not only had given Scott seiki, she instilled in him the confidence of believing he was capable of doing anything with his life.

Years after Osumi Sensei had watched Brad give seiki to many people and had visited his home several times, Brad had a visionary experience much like the one Sensei had as a young girl. A white snake jumped into his belly. He watched it sprout out of him as a Bodhi tree that, in turn, had a heart-shaped leaf that blossomed into the Buddha.

*These things are not to be explained, nor are they to be given any discourse that frames them as anything other than the movement of seiki. The only miracle is that we can become fully alive. Seiki is simply a name for the awakening of this immediate realization. How it manifests may be formulated in an infinite number of ways. Whatever we experience is always a poem, a truth whose metaphors are wrapped in layers of ever-transforming meanings. In the ceaseless movement of meanings, metaphor finds life—the seiki of poetic, improvisational living. As the Tree of Life expresses the heart of all that stands rooted to the ground with arms stretching and waving at the sky, a fruit drops from the perfect bud-of-nature. In the crossing back and forth is found the middle way, the Buddha of being neither human nor god. Rather than ponder*

*it, rather than contemplate contemplation, stand up and reach for the fruit of another tree. Drink the luminous mystery, the elixir of youth poured by the wisdom of age.*

Brad did not immediately report his vision of the white snake to Osumi Sensei, but soon after, she called from Japan saying she had to see him again. She and her entourage flew to the United States; she emerged from the plane in traditional dress. That evening she told everyone in our party the story of how the lineage of seiki is passed on. Whenever anyone is given the responsibility of carrying on seiki jutsu, the priests at her ancestor's shrine prepare a special piece of wood with this person's name written on it and then make prayers to bless the event. She handed Brad a rectangular piece of wood with his name on it. It was wrapped with two antique pieces of silk that were the only possessions she had from her aunt's lineage. She said, "You are to teach everyone about this way of living with seiki. You are to carry on this tradition."

She handed Brad a written letter signed by her and cosigned by her daughter, Masako, who served as a witness, giving Brad the authority to teach the tradition of seiki jutsu to others. It states:

October 12, 1996

To Whom It May Concern:

I, Ikuko Osumi, acknowledge that I have chosen Bradford Keeney, Ph.D., as one of my successors and that I entrust to him the role of representing and overseeing the teaching of seiki jutsu as well as the transmission to others . . .

Sincerely,

Ikuko Osumi

Witness Signature:

Masako Hayashibe

She later wrote:

Dear Professor Keeney,
I have entire trust in you and in whatever you do.
I leave all the activities related to seiki entirely to you.
I am appreciative to you as always.
With love,
Ikuko Osumi

Brad was deeply honored, but shocked to receive the wood, silk cloth, and legal document that made him a successor. Brad felt the confidence Osumi Sensei had in him, and her continued support and encouragement enabled him to feel the authority to teach seiki jutsu. She had been like a second mother to Brad in helping nurture both seiki and his confidence in its natural expression. Just as her aunt had encouraged her to practice seiki, Osumi Sensei supported Brad's becoming a master of seiki jutsu.

As Osumi's aunt said, there are no words that can explain seiki. There is nothing that can be understood about seiki that will help you bring it forth. You must experience it. When you wonder whether you have experienced it, you haven't. However, when you finally do feel seiki, you will know it without a doubt. Seiki is non-subtle. Osumi Sensei would laugh when she'd say that "any practice that calls itself a 'subtle energy work' has no seiki." She believed that the concept of "subtle energy" was invented as a marketing ploy to help sell something that is typically not there. If it is truly the vital life force, it is non-subtle. Furthermore, in this work there are few masters. Although everyone can have his or her life transformed and energized by seiki, it is ludicrous to imagine promising multitudes that they can become seiki masters. Her raw honesty about these matters was uncompromising. Osumi said that "so-called subtle energy practitioners were often so subtle that there was either no energy or no practitioner in its practice."

When a person becomes a master of seiki, she develops an understanding of how seiki moves along a line or river, and that a master must make a connection with these "seiki lines" as Osumi Sensei called them. Even the relationship between a seiki master and a client has a seiki line connecting the two where the seiki flows. Osumi Sensei said that line is what taught her and called to her when she healed. Osumi Sensei was delighted to learn from Brad that the Kalahari Bushmen and other ecstatic healing traditions also know these lines or ropes, which are the pathways for the vital life force.

*These lines and ropes connect all beings, and most importantly they connect us to the source of creation—what some have called the rope to God. These lines are the streams, rivers, and channels through which seiki passes. They function like telephone lines—enabling heightened communication—and like power lines delivering the force of life. These lines, only perceived through the awakened spiritual senses, are found inside the spiritual universe, where high-frequency vibrations make materiality less relevant. Here the heart holds the universe and the mind is found at home inside it.*

When Osumi Sensei introduced Brad to two of her clients—Dr. Kato, the inventor of the DVD, and Dr. Toshi Doi, one of the inventors of the CD—they told Brad they were inventing a supersensitive microphone capable of detecting the vital life force. Brad demonstrated how other traditions handle seiki, and they were very pleased to learn everything they could about what they regard as the next major frontier in science. For these renowned scientists, seiki was a known fact of the universe, and they were studying it in their laboratory.

When Brad first met Osumi Sensei in 1992, she told him that he had spontaneously received a full transmission of seiki in 1970. An undergraduate student at the time, he had walked into a university chapel where he suddenly felt a mysterious force enter his body—the experience changed his whole life. Osumi Sensei knew this about Brad before he talked about it with her. She explained what other healers from around the world had told him: The rarest and strongest way of receiving a full transmission of the vital life force is one that takes place spontaneously without another person mediating its delivery. Many cultures regard such a recipient as a gifted healer and teacher. There is no ego or jealousy about this, but only respect and happiness over the realization that someone has been "made" this way and is available to help others.

When he was a university student, Brad experimented with musical improvisation, tinkering with ways to open his heart so music could readily flow. He developed his own way of "playing the piano with feelings." He had grown up in the country churches of his father and grandfather, where he was a devoted practitioner of his faith. The day of his energetic awakening, Brad had been at a record shop and found himself walking out of it for no reason at all. He felt a deep peace and calm come over him. His walking was automatic and spontaneous, without conscious purpose—it felt as though he was outside the field of gravity and was floating along the sidewalk. His body walked him into the university chapel, where he sat down in the first pew. Then a ball of energy came to life in his belly. Like a volcano releasing molten lava, the vital life force released and climbed slowly up his spine. As it rose it felt like it was giving birth to multiple hearts. He felt many hearts beating in his body as the energy kept rising. All this was taking place spontaneously to a young man who had never read about kundalini or spiritual awakenings like this. He was outside of cognition or commentary. He surrendered to the experience.

As the vital life force ascended, Brad began to weep with joy, for this was the most ecstatic happiness and love he had ever known. His heart seemed to grow as large as the universe; he understood that all of life was an interpenetrating unity. As the life force came out of the top of his head, it transformed into a large, oval, egg-like luminosity that stood in front of him. Inside this holy light he witnessed and felt the presence of religious masters: Jesus, the Virgin Mary, Buddha, and others. It was a psychosynesthetic experience—all the senses combined and amplified so that he could see, hear, and even taste his feelings. Brad felt as if a downloading of wisdom and know-how was taking place. He was being rewired and made into someone different, prepared for a new way of being in the world. He trembled and shook throughout the experience and felt heat permeate his body. The visionary experience lasted through the entire night; the next morning when he left the chapel he had to keep his gaze lowered to the ground lest the light return and overtake him again in its infinite embrace.

Being a science nerd, the first thing Brad did was walk straight to a bookstore to see if he could find a book that would explain his experience. A book literally fell off a shelf in front of him; picking it up Brad noticed that it was the autobiography of Gopi Krishna. In that book he read about kundalini and the vital life force for the first time in his life. In the days and weeks that followed, rather than tell anyone what happened, Brad followed the inner voice and visionary dreams that came to him. From that day forward Brad was full of seiki, and he spontaneously did what masters of the life force do—he let himself be led by the energetic force inside him, which always took him where he most needed to go. He became a student of cybernetics, a scientific orientation that helped him see human experience primarily as circular interaction rather than psychological process. This helped free him from the head tripping that interferes with spontaneous presence in everyday life. His dreams led him to healers all over the world, including Osumi Sensei in Japan.

During the 1990s, Osumi Sensei oversaw Brad's many explorations of how seiki was practiced around the world. He became acknowledged as a healer and spiritual teacher in numerous cultural healing traditions. Most noteworthy, Brad became a "Heart of the Spears" *n/om kxao,* the strongest level of healer among the Kalahari Bushmen. Osumi Sensei told Brad how his life would unfold, saying there would be great difficulties and challenges that included various injustices brought on by jealousy and human cruelty, as it had been for her and her ancestral relations.

Osumi Sensei believed that we are each born with a mission or purpose. Seiki helps us find our destiny. When several spiritual seekers asked Osumi Sensei why Brad had been chosen to succeed her rather than the others who had worked so hard as her deshi, she simply replied, "It is his destiny." Seiki's truest teaching is to allow life to move us and lead us to become what is naturally intended. Our usual modus operandi is to feel removed from the improvisational flow of seiki. When the vital life force fully enters us, we become what we are meant to be. Then and only then do we find true happiness and peace. With seiki jutsu we are tuned and connected with the dynamic pulse of life.

Osumi Sensei told Brad that a day would come when he would find a true partner with whom he could share this lineage and healing way. She said to him, "It will be difficult to patiently wait for your time, because there are so many things you are being taught from around the world. Seiki will be the bridge that helps bring these different teachings together. You will suffer, but you must endure and wait for the right time to successfully establish seiki jutsu in the world. You cannot do this work alone. No one can do it alone. You must do it with a partner. I promise that this day will come. You will know when you and your partner are ready to hold the teaching of seiki."

In 2009, we (Brad and Hillary) met when we were assigned to teach a university class together in San Francisco. One night before classes began, some of the students hosted a late-night gathering that included music and ecstatic movement. By that time many of the students were familiar with Brad's way of doing ecstatic seiki work with groups, so they asked Brad to be present. Hillary had never before witnessed Brad work in this way and knew little about his history as a healer, but on this evening she felt particularly drawn to attend since they were going to be teaching together. She sat down in a chair in the corner. Brad felt automatically pulled to come over and place his vibrating hands on her head, though in the darkness he was not aware of who it was that he was touching. Immediately Hillary felt a kind of electric peace wash over her. She experienced all thoughts fall away, as if she was filled with empty space.

Brad then opened his arms to embrace Hillary. Seiki immediately flowed between us. Brad felt transported to the Kalahari, as if he were holding a Bushman healer; he also felt that Osumi Sensei was giving us seiki. With Brad still not knowing who he was holding, we stayed connected to each other, vibrating this way for several hours. When the gathering finally ended and the lights came on, we were surprised to find ourselves embraced in a vibrating seiki hug.

In that instant we knew our lives would never be the same. We threw away our course plan and created a class that evoked and fostered spontaneous transformation. Students began having spiritual experiences, and transmissions of seiki took place, even though the course was conducted online and nothing was explicitly taught about seiki. The course was renamed "Cooking the Silver Trout," inspired by the Yeats poem "The Song of Wandering Aengus," which had become a major theme in the class: *"I went out to the hazel wood / Because a fire was in my head . . . And hooked a berry to a thread . . . And caught a little silver trout . . . It had become a glimmering girl / With apple blossom in her hair . . ."*

*Seiki masters and Bushman doctors know that seiki awakens a fire in your belly that travels up to the heart and out the top of your head. When this happens you automatically reach for the embrace of another, so that the seiki can flow between you. This is how doctors make each other's seiki strong. Again from Yeats, "Though I am old with wandering / Through hollow lands and hilly lands, / I will find out where she has gone / And kiss her lips and take her hands . . ."* Seiki is a fire that feeds on love.

After the course was over, Brad took Hillary to look for a piece of jewelry in the shape of a fish that could be a necklace for her, in celebration of our new relationship. The first store we entered was the legendary Gump's in San Francisco, and to our surprise the attendant said that they had something special in their vault that had been collected many years ago in Japan. She returned with a fish made out of the same steel that was used to make a samurai sword. It had been the sole piece of jewelry worn on a belt around the waist by a Japanese woman in the 1800s. Brad remembered how Osumi Sensei wore that same type of jewelry when she was dressed in her kimono.

Prior to meeting Brad, Hillary had spent five years living at the Zen Center of Los Angeles, with evening sojourns to nearby salsa and tango dance floors. Following a long involvement in community activism, Hillary turned her interest to studying what underlies the artistry of facilitating personal and relational change. Her research on cybernetics, Zen koans, and creative transformation brought her close to the heart of Brad's work. They became partners dedicated to bringing contemporary forms of transformation and spiritual renewal into relationships with the healing ways held inside great wisdom traditions.

Shortly after they met and committed to their life and work together, Brad and Hillary received word that a benefactor wanted to help their mission. Once the largest financial contributor to Transcendental Meditation, the movement responsible for helping bring meditation to the West, this benefactor had made a prayer asking if there was a wisdom teaching the world should know about. The next day he found Brad's book *Bushman Shaman* misfiled on a shelf in a Boulder bookstore. Reading the book set his heart on fire; he contacted Brad, saying he wanted our work to be more available to the world.

With these auspicious blessings, we soon married and became partners in carrying the seiki jutsu lineage into the future. In 2012 we started The Keeney Institute for Healing, dedicated to promoting and advancing ecstatic healing and spirituality, especially seiki jutsu, the Japanese art of working with the non-subtle vital life force. As a self-healing and revitalization practice, we teach how spontaneous and effortless action provides the most natural means for tuning, awakening, and transforming your life. The Keeney Institute for Healing, based in New Orleans, Louisiana, with special programs all over the world, offers special events, private sessions, and a two-year mentorship program. Basic instruction in the daily seiki jutsu practice of self-healing and renewal, along with immersion in "seiki conversation," helps clients prepare for a reception of enhanced seiki. We guide clients through the stages of seiki development and provide teaching for how the vital life force can infuse everyday life.

Whether it is called seiki, n/om, kundalini, or chi, among other possible names, seiki points to an essential quality that underlies the flow experience, creative expression, and here-and-now presence. We teach that no method of performance, spiritual practice, therapeutic orientation, or philosophy of life can fully awaken unless you are instilled with sufficient seiki. With seiki jutsu you find the key to daily well-being and extraordinary living. This work is what Osumi Sensei and other healers have asked and blessed to take place. We are dedicated to fulfilling this mission.

We have seen people from all walks of life, including mothers, fathers, insurance agents, interior decorators, musicians, school teachers, nurses, doctors, engineers, waitresses, clerks, painters, poets, carpenters, and computer programmers, to name a few, have profound spiritual experiences that were initiated by allowing their bodies to be spontaneously moved by seiki. As we have seen time and time again, no matter what spiritual tradition you belong to, or even if you do not adopt any particular tradition, the natural movements of spontaneous expression can carry you into a spiritual experience that may completely alter your life.

"I have given you a glimpse of seiki, the vital life force," Osumi Sensei told Brad. "You should not live without it. It brings true fulfillment to your life. It is like the tide of the sea that approaches to satisfy and quench the thirst of seashore sand. Thanks to seiki we can maintain our health and embrace each other peacefully, respectfully, and forgivingly. It brings about a generous frame of mind. This generous mind asks that we nurture and prosper with seiki, benefiting ourselves and the universe at the same time. The door to seiki is open to everyone who wishes to enter."

# 3

## SEIKI JUTSU

### The Transmission of Seiki

A ll this time, while you have been on a journey looking for a greater truth—whatever words you use to describe it, seiki has been hunting you. It has tracked your every move. No matter what happens to you—happiness, sadness, health, sickness, victory, or defeat—seiki understands that all of it is making you ready to receive the ultimate gift. You are being softened, tenderized, and seasoned, readied for a new birth, an entry into vital, sanctified living. Until you are filled with seiki, something will be missing in your life.

A lightning bolt of seiki has already formed, made especially made for you. It's already hanging in the sky waiting to shoot itself into your heart. The divine mystery is pulling back the bow; its string is made of your life, and it holds the lightning arrow of seiki that can awaken the original mysteries. Prepare to stand softly and tenderly and become completely available under the sky as the clouds gather for a special delivery. Become a lightning rod for God's arrow, the seiki bolt that has you in its sight.

Get struck by seiki and find yourself coming home. Stop wandering aimlessly; instead, let seiki take aim. You are the bull's eye. Show yourself. Look up to the sky and tell all of creation that you are ready to receive its holiest gift. You are tired and weary, or at least some part of you wants to go further in this relatively brief journey of life. Maybe you're just doing it for your children, so that seiki will stay alive in the next generation. You need to be touched by the eternal. There is no time to waste. It's time for you to meet seiki and receive the true secret to a vital and fulfilled life.

---

Osumi Sensei believed that the most important gift a person can receive is seiki. She isn't alone with this assessment of what is most important in life. The Kalahari Bushmen teach the same thing. When we forget about seiki we easily get lost and think that what we need most in our lives is some kind of conceptual belief or understanding—whether it's spiritual, psychological, economic, or scientific. We act as if there is a right answer and solution to our questions and problems, but nothing could be further from the truth. The most important life-changing transformations take place when seiki is flowing through your whole being; without seiki, even the deepest and most profound thoughts cannot mobilize us to live fully. It is seiki that you are looking for, whether or not you know it. The great news is that the greatest truths are delivered with ecstatic joy! With seiki, any thought or practice can come alive. You will feel a resonance within that brings on a sudden and heightened emotion of delight.

Though anyone can be prepared to receive seiki, few are ready for it to fully enter. Why is this? What are the preconditions to fully receiving seiki? The Bushmen say that you must be sufficiently "softened" in order for the highly charged life force to successfully fill you up. If you need to be softened in order to receive seiki, then what constructs the armor that impedes or prevents its entry? Whenever you elevate the workings of mind, thought, and language over heart, feelings, and emotive expression, you risk losing the softness required for seiki to enter. When the ego and the narrating mind become the frame that holds and organizes your daily living, you too easily minimize (or analyze) feelings and the heart-full presence that inspires play, absurdity, music, dance, and creativity. Getting soft means lifting metaphor over literality, play over piety, absurdity over rationality, spontaneous performance over routine habit, invention over reproduction, effortless action over willed action, unconscious over conscious mentation, and most importantly, love over power. The heart is limitless and is the transportation hub of the heavens. Metaphorically speaking, your mind must live inside of your heart, rather than making heart live inside mind.

At the same time, if you are too frivolous and don't take the performance of your life seriously enough, you can build an insensitivity and carelessness that is as hard and resistant to the life force as someone who is zealously pious and naively rule-bound. "Getting soft" values how words can evoke wisdom, poetry, and clarity and encourages us to be natural scholars as well as natural lovers. Softness is both disciplined and imaginative. It can discern and learn, say "no" and "whoa" in order to grow, be bold and not always have to be told what to hold, and arrange to be found in order to reach higher ground. Softness is not found in what you think about things or even in your shifting emotional barometer, but in how you relate to all your experiences and in your ability to move with constant change, interpenetration, and metamorphosis.

The Bushmen regard the mind and its handling of language as the domain of the trickster. They are suspicious of trickster, or what we can call trickster mind, for it delights in being clever and tricky without giving equal respect and importance to our gut feelings and heart-filled emotions. Authentic ecstatic shamans won't ask you to give a report on what you know. They will ask you to sing a song, knowing that your heart will be revealed when you sing. They know that talk can be deceptive, while music is more revealing of your heart and how soft you are.

At the same time, it is important not to place trickster inside a duality that makes it out to be an enemy that needs to be silenced or destroyed. For the Bushmen, trickster is one of the faces of God and can be helpful at times—but as the Bushmen warn, be careful, for it can change course at any moment. Utilize the trickster nature of mind to counter the trickster nature of mind. If this is paradoxical, then be paradoxical about it. Don't be hard on your mind; soften it instead. Tickle your ego and giggle at its curmudgeonly sense of self-importance. Thank it for making you distinct and truly one-of-a-kind. This will help you become more malleable and resilient when it comes to notions of thought, deed, and emotion.

When you are sufficiently soft, you are ready for the seiki lines to  be hooked up so the life force can travel through them like a major conduit or pipeline. As the Bushmen would say, when you are soft an arrow of n/om can pierce you. Similarly, parishioners in the sanctified Black church speak of one being readied to receive the holy spirit when the "heart is right." This readiness does not mean mindlessness or an anti-intellectual mindset, but a change in the relationship of mind to  heart. Here mind and language serve to maintain what the Zen masters call beginner's mind, a ripened and seasoned childlike presence that is responsive to the longings and callings of love and joyful engagement in acts of creative expression.

⁂

*Don't try too hard to be soft. Don't worry about whether you're soft enough or analyze why your cranky neighbor received an arrow of seiki without even looking for one, when you've been waiting patiently on your best spiritual behavior. Your trickster mind will likely be surprised to find out that being soft and available for seiki has little to do with how much you meditate, what you eat, how socially just or environmentally responsible you are, how many spiritual books you read, or whether you can read at all. Though we can truthfully say that things like a generous spirit, a belly full of laughter, a love for God, or a heart broken by suffering will help soften you, it's just as important to remember that spiritual matters are complex and beyond understanding. Become softened by accepting that which is impossible to measure or easy to define.*

There are two ways of receiving seiki when you are soft and ready. The first way is the rarest form, no matter what culture it takes place in. It occurs when a person spontaneously receives seiki without asking. The Bushmen, who have the longest history of working with seiki, observe that this usually only happens to a person who is between 18 and 21 years of age. They believe that the Creator or Sky God chooses a few people for direct spiritual transmission. Similarly, few are chosen to experience a direct transmission of seiki unmediated by another human being. When God transmits seiki, it is a special preparation for creating a spiritual teacher and healer who has a direct seiki pipeline to the original mysteries.

The strongest masters of seiki jutsu receive a direct transmission, and they in turn can help develop other seiki masters and teachers. These mentored teachers are also able to transmit seiki to others. Both kinds of master practitioners—those who receive direct transmission and those who are mentored by another teacher—are able to help others get soft and ready for seiki. When we help people get soft, we tease them with absurdity, allowing laughter and play to balance any overly serious search for interpretive meaning. Laughter not only provides good medicine, it spiritually offers your mind a good housecleaning. Be careful about trying to figure things out, for seeking insight can cause spiritual blindness. Find a way to awaken your spiritual senses. You need spiritual vision, hearing, smell, taste, and feeling in order to navigate the most important journeys. These spiritual senses only spring to life when you are plugged into seiki.

You are softened when you hang out in situations where the atmosphere has high spiritual voltage. We are fond of sanctified churches, though they are not so easy to find anymore. If you didn't grow up in one or have never experienced one yourself, take another look at the scene of the Black church service with James Brown in the *Blues Brothers* movie and you can get a feel for what we are talking about. Find the kind of soulful music and rhythms that charge your existential batteries. A seiki master knows how to supercharge the room, theatre, or auditorium with electrified seiki. You can feel it in the air. There is quite literally a glow to the room that can be seen when seiki enters. We once worked with a group that included a family with an adolescent boy. He exclaimed, "I can't believe it! The room changed!" That's how it is when seiki charges the atmosphere.

Seiki masters also help soften and prepare you to receive seiki by working with your problems and suffering. Seiki masters are gifted with the ability to work with the kinds of issues or concerns that you have wondered about taking to a therapist, counselor, or coach. Bring your troubles to a seiki master, and she will work with them as a means of softening you. We conduct seiki sessions for individuals, couples, and families, doing so to get them ready for revitalized living. "Getting doctored" by a seiki master is part of the process of transformation and preparation for transmission.

Old-school healers regard symptoms, problems, and suffering as gifts that provide a "soft spot," a place in which an opening can be made for seiki. As Mother Teresa said, all suffering is a spiritual teaching and a gift. Rather than fight suffering, find a way to communicate and cooperate with it so its gift can be received. Here we find that healing goes past both problem solving and solution finding. Seiki sees both the denotation of a problem and a solution as masking what is underneath—the gift that these experiences bring to helping open the flow of seiki in your life and relationships.

When you are soft and ready for seiki, a seiki master will feel it. At this time you will be given a highly charged and concentrated bolt of seiki. It can take place in a group gathering, in a specially created ceremony, or spontaneously without announcement. A seiki master has no need for a fixed protocol. Transmission can happen automatically, even when it is scheduled. What remains consistent is that the transmission of seiki will always involve ecstatic sound making, spontaneous movement, and seiki-charged expression.

In a transmission, the room is first charged with seiki; this typically involves making percussive sounds. Osumi Sensei banged the walls. We have used drumming or our own voices to get things stirring. Seiki sounds are then shot from the mouth, sounding like hissing, long drawn-out sounds, shrieks, and shouts. All of this is critical for amplifying seiki—it activates the spontaneity of the transmitter and recipient, and it amplifies seiki in the room.

As the seiki energy builds, it will approach a crescendo. At that moment the seiki master's hands are automatically drawn to the top of the recipient's head. There are times when the atmosphere is so concentrated with seiki it feels as if the seiki can be grabbed and wiped on the recipient's head. The seiki can feel like taffy, honey, or it can feel like a wet stream; in fact, seiki feels like it can change into any form at all—solid, liquid, or vapor. When the seiki master's hands are on the recipient's head, seiki enters through the top of the head. It flows down the spine in a purposeful and certain manner, traveling all the way to the base of the spine and filling the recipient with seiki.

Once filled with seiki, you will always be filled. However, with seiki jutsu we often say that it can fill you more than 100 percent. You can be made to overflow. When a master or teacher gives you seiki, we want you to be at least 110 percent filled. We know how much goes into you because we feel it at the same time. As it goes into you, it goes into us. It does this if and only if we are in the highest vibratory relationship with it. This is why singing and movement is so important. It is next to impossible for a transmitter of seiki to get sufficiently charged without ecstatic sound making. With vibratory sound, the seiki is attracted like lightning to a lightning rod. At this point the song and the seiki line are the same. When seiki is attracted to a song, seiki becomes the song. Seiki songs—also called n/om songs, shamanic songs, or holy ghost songs in other cultures—are seiki attractor songs. When seiki flows through them they become seiki songs, seiki lines, and song lines.

A person's reaction to receiving seiki can vary. Some have dramatic encounters and start shaking. Others have gentle rocking movements, while a few have more of an internal sensation. All forms of response are equal and a more explicitly dramatic reaction does not necessarily mean that more seiki was received. If you are sufficiently soft, you won't be attached to what form of expression you think should be enacted. What is important is to allow spontaneity to come forth naturally and effortlessly. In a way, softening is training to become spontaneous. When you are comfortable with spontaneous expression, it can more naturally take place. Though there is more to seiki than this, it is important to remember that seiki always brings forth effortless, non-purposeful movement, both internally and externally.

Once seiki is instilled, it is not uncommon for the recipient to go into an automatic motion such as rocking. After a few minutes of doing this, the seiki master may tap or pat the base of the client's spine to bring closure to the transmission. In the Japanese tradition of seiki jutsu, this is when the master makes the announcement, "Congratulations, you have received seiki." For a Bushman, the community will say "Congratulations, you have received an arrow or nail of n/om." In a sanctified church you will hear, "Congratulations, you had a baptism in the holy spirit." Other places might discuss transmissions of kundalini or chi or simply say that a transmission has taken place. The name matters less than the ecstatic experience that fostered natural movement.

It is important to recognize that a transmission of seiki is more than a routinized ritual, which is what many presumed "spiritual transmissions" often are. You will know that seiki has been transmitted because it will surge within you and begin awakening the original mysteries of spirituality—the complete range of mystical (and shamanic) experiences—over the course of the rest of your life, especially if you maintain your daily practice. We have seen people's lives changed by seiki. After studying religions, spiritualities, healing practices, and transformative paths all over the world, we can say that there is nothing like receiving seiki. It is the experience that rewires you to have access to the vital life force. With it, any practice and way of knowing can come to life.

We now offer some glimpses of clients who have received a transmission of seiki. They come from varied backgrounds, ages, and cultures. Each person's life prospered because they were all able to receive seiki and build their connection and relationship to this vital life force.

It is June 1997, and Brad is conducting a demonstration before an audience of psychotherapists and medical doctors in Belo Horizonte, Brazil. A volunteer, a distinguished psychoanalyst in her early fifties, is sitting on the bench, waiting for Brad to instill seiki. As often happens, Brad feels Osumi Sensei by his side; he can hear her making ecstatic sounds as he claps his hands. A heavy vibration starts oscillating at the base of his spine. It launches itself upward as his body shakes with the electrical-like impact. "Ahh-hi! Ahh-hi-hi!" Brad's voice exclaims, while his arms whirl about spontaneously.

Soon the motion begins slowing down, becoming gentle while at the same time increasing in intensity. Now the least visible movements carry the highest frequencies and bring the most concentrated current. Every once in a while a jolt of concentrated seiki kicks everything into high gear, like shifting gears in a racing car. This cycle of amplification continues—big jolts trigger more finely tuned trembling, carrying energy that has been further amplified.

As Brad is overflowing with seiki, he feels all his spiritual mentors around him. They are assisting in the creation of a swirling wind of seiki that enters the room like a tornado. It moves over the woman's head, ready to touch down. Its powerful wind lifts Brad's hands and drops them over her head. At that moment of contact the room changes. There are no longer walls, floor, or ceiling. The cosmos has opened and Brad feels himself hovering over the woman in a place where gravity no longer rules. Waves of seiki, n/om, the vital life force, holy spirit, chi, kundalini are in synch with the waves of rippling muscles in his torso.

One crescendo after another voices itself with sound and movem
With each round the energy continues to build. A storm is in the m.
ing. Something is being released from above.

Brad closes his eyes and sees white clouds rolling in. Soon lightning
may strike. He knows it will because he has the certainty that comes
from long experience with seiki. The sounds are pulsing, a thunderous
rumble is building, and then more enhanced seiki arrives effortlessly
and spontaneously. There is a crackling of newborn energy inside both
of their spines. What she feels, Brad also feels with her. They share
this experience as enhanced seiki flows through both of them. They
are whipped from one side to another by an unseen vortex of energy
that continues entering the top of the woman's head and extends to the
furthest edge of the great vastness of eternity. Seiki is shooting down
through the atmosphere. Sunshine is filling the room with illumination. She and Brad are both shining from the luminosity seiki brings.

*Into the seiki dreamtime you fall, arms wrapped around a new-
born spirit. You are stretched across two oceans, pulled so far that
you become elongated until you are nothing but a thin line, a line
of light extending between Grandmother Africa and Grandmother
Asia. To the north and south, and in all points in between, you
see other lines stretching across dowsing rods, shaking tents, gyrat-
ing bodies in a holy ghost dance, musicians being played by the
music—all manifestations of the same current.*

*With a quivering body, you reach to hold hands with both the
longed-for Mother below and Father above. Unchoreographed,
unrehearsed, this childlike quest seeks marriage of wildest movement and deepest stillness. You plunge headfirst into the immediate mystery, juggling life and death. A voice is heard amidst the
stars, "The lines are circles and the circles, when moved, become
the Wheel. Feel the wind, the current, the spirit. This is seiki."*

A couple come to see us for help with their marriage. They arrive for a weekend stay and we see them each morning and afternoon. On the second day, seiki fills the room. It sometimes does that without notice—when a client is ready, seiki arrives. Get soft and seiki will come. We hold their hands and begin moving them, so seiki can find their soft spot and release its gift. Seiki touches us first, as it always does, and soon we begin to shout and sing.

Our hands automatically go to the top of the husband's head. He starts yelling: "This is unbelievable! It feels like you are pouring sacred botanicals into me. Are you wiping mushrooms on my head? What is this?" He becomes intoxicated with the seiki that is being poured into him.

The man, who is a businessman and had only come because his wife asked him to, cannot stop shouting words of appreciation, wonder, and gratitude. He starts visioning and feels that he is being reborn. Even after he leaves the session, he continues to feel intoxicated during the week following.

*A voice is heard in the streets: "The lines are circles and the circles, when moved, become the Wheel. Feel the wind, the current, the spirit. Drink it. This is seiki."*

Even a child can receive seiki. When Brad's son was twelve years old, Brad said a silent bedtime prayer for him. He always sang Scott a couple of songs and then they'd recite a bedtime prayer together before tucking him in. Before turning off his bedroom light, Brad silently prayed, "Dear Lord, please give Scott a special gift tonight. Show him that there is a true world of spiritual mystery. Let him know there is more to life than Nike shoes and action figures. Please reveal what is important. Thank you." Brad then placed his hand on Scott's head and seiki began to move into the room. Not wanting to startle Scott, while at the same time knowing that seiki had a mind of its own, Brad allowed the seiki to build up in the room. It filled Brad with so much spiritual electricity that he was soon unable to hold it in any longer. In an instant, a lightning bolt shot through Brad and went out of his hand into Scott's head. Scott did not make a sound; he had fallen sound asleep. Brad looked around and saw the room lit up with a soft glowing luminosity. He knew that some kind of transmission had taken place. Seiki had passed between him and his son. Brad wept while offering a prayer of gratitude, and then went to bed.

At two in the morning, Brad was awakened by the sound of Scott screaming out loud from his room. "Dad, Dad, get in here! Get in here Dad!" Brad jumped out of his bed and ran to the next room. Scott was sitting up in bed looking shocked. "Dad, I don't know what happened. I was wide awake and something happened."

"What happened, Scott?" Brad asked. "Tell me about it."

"It was like I was walking down the street and then all of a sudden something took hold of me and carried me up into the sky. I kept going up until I got to the highest place. There I met God. He told me how everything works."

At that moment Scott started yawning and tucking himself under the covers. Brad couldn't resist asking, "What did God say?" Scott replied, "I'm too tired now, Dad." He then fell back asleep. Brad never asked Scott again about what happened that night because some things are too sacred to talk about or put in words.

Ever since that night, Scott, professionally known as DJ Skee, has been fearless and has believed that he can do practically anything. All he has to do is try, and what needs to happen eventually comes forth. He graduated from high school a year early, didn't go to college, and started working for the president of Loud Records in Hollywood when he was 18. When he was 28 years old, *Billboard* magazine cited him as one of the top 30 under-30 entrepreneurs in the entertainment industry. Seiki is no stranger to happy endings.

Brad once gave seiki to over 500 people in an all-day ceremony in California. A line formed and, one by one, he laid his hands on each person and let seiki do its thing. One of the recipients was a world-famous classical pianist. He immediately saw a great light appear that poured into him. He jumped with joy and hugged Brad, while lifting him up with glee. Seiki supercharged his music, and his performances later had an energy that critics could not explain.

The same thing happened to the president of an international college with whom we worked. When seiki was transmitted to him, he witnessed a luminosity that entered his body. He felt "illumined inside his brain," to use his words, and it lasted for weeks. Seiki changed his life, and he became dedicated to bringing more of the vital life force to his university. Seiki brings a new kind of graduation—it signals the beginning of a life that walks in spiritual light.

One of seiki's most interesting clients was Dr. Bertrand Piccard from Lausanne, Switzerland. He came from a family of famous adventurers and record-breaking engineers and scientists. His grandfather Auguste helped establish modern aviation in the 1930s through his invention of the pressurized air cabin and stratospheric balloon. In 1931 he became the first human being to enter Earth's stratosphere after ascending 16,000 feet in his invention. Bertrand's father, Jacques, was an oceanographer who developed underwater vehicles. He holds the world record for the deepest underwater dive.

Continuing in his family's pioneering footsteps, Dr. Piccard attempted what many thought was an impossible feat—flying around the world nonstop in a hot air balloon. He attempted it several times but found that he didn't have enough energy and stamina to get all the way around the globe. Then he invited Brad to host a seiki jutsu event at his private villa in Switzerland.

To Brad's surprise, Dr. Piccard, a medical doctor, had a device that supposedly could measure the range of one's vital energy. Whereas other energy practitioners had a range of several feet, Picard's instrument continued to respond even when Brad was walking around outside the villa. Brad gave everyone seiki and taught Piccard about seiki. That year, 1999, Dr. Picard became the first human being to fly nonstop around the globe in a balloon. He sent Brad a thank-you for the energy that helped him make history.

Seiki can do more than take you around the world. In New York City, at the Open Center, Brad placed his hands on the head of a Tibetan monk and gave him seiki. The energetic exchange was so strong that the man was propelled backward while sitting in a chair. Literally, he and his chair did a backward somersault. He immediately went into an ecstasy, shouting with joy that he was seeing the Divine Mother, an illumination that infused remarkable spiritual energy into his life.

In another situation, an engineer came with his wife to a seiki intensive. He did not want to go to the event and was skeptical. He introduced himself as someone who didn't believe in seiki and said he would likely leave before the morning was over. Brad asked him to stay through lunch so he could at least witness seiki being given to someone else. He agreed. Brad decided to show an old film made by John Marshall, the first recording made of a Bushman transmitting the life force. It was a black-and-white film and was not of good quality. During the film, Brad became full of seiki, something not uncommon for him. As a Bushman was shown being shot with vital force energy, Brad let out a loud seiki shout. In that instant, the engineer felt something strike him, and he fell out of his chair. Brad went to him and placed his hands on the man's head. Seiki flowed into him.

The engineer was not prepared for what would happen to him. He entered a visionary state and saw things that would happen that day in the lives of others. He also felt an energy pour through him that made him shout with delight. That evening he watched the news and everything he had seen in the vision was reported. He received more visions and clairvoyance all night and continued doing so for months. He became one of our students, and today he is a healer, someone who is able to handle seiki.

In a small town in Louisiana, two Christian ministers allowed us to give them seiki. Both experienced the holy spirit in a way they had never known before. They startled trembling and feeling electricity charge through their body. One of the preachers had a sacred vision that night. God came to him in the dream and said, "You had known me and committed yourself to me, but had not yet consummated our relationship." Seiki brought him closer to God. He could feel holiness living inside of him after seiki.

Is seiki the holy spirit, or vice versa? Don't ask the question. No one knows how to explain any spiritual mystery, especially the source that awakens us to encounter holiness. The name is less important than the experience. And the experience is beyond the grasp of any name or understanding.

The other minister received seiki and trembled for hours. He believed the holy spirit was baptizing him in an experience he had only read about but had not yet experienced firsthand. It changed his life and he became a professor of counseling in a religious college where he is dedicated to teaching practitioners to emphasize accessing the holy spirit over employing psychological methods for counsel and healing. Seiki is a spiritual gas station. Pull yourself up to its pump and fill yourself up. It will change your life by bringing more life to your living.

Once we met a business executive at a seiki intensive; on the very first morning we could tell he was soft enough for seiki. When we started to work instilling seiki, the room immediately turned into a seiki storm and the life force entered the man, doing so as it had for the clients of Osumi and as it had for the Bushmen in the Kalahari. He began weeping with joy and felt himself transported to another place and time. He could smell his grandfather's scent even though his grandfather had passed away many years before. He was also introduced to his other ancestors, including a departed sister, in a deeply heartfelt connection. Today this man is a devoted practitioner of seiki. He has helped us give seiki to others, and we know that his life will continue to meet more mysteries that are awakened by seiki.

You don't need a holy ceremonial ground to transmit seiki. Aɪ place at all will do as long as the seiki lines are lined up correctly and the moment is right. An aikido practitioner was spontaneously given seiki by Brad in a driveway in Albuquerque, New Mexico. Don tells the story:

Dark clouds began to fill the sky and we were both startled by a clap of lightning. Suddenly I realized that he [Brad] was trembling throughout his body. He began to place his hand on my chest and move me in various ways with an unbelievable high energy. At the same time he produced strange wind/jungle/animal sounds interspersed with bursts of excited exclamations in an unidentifiable, primitive sounding language and in a voice that did not seem to be his own.

I am not sure how long this experience lasted because I seemed to have entered a dreamlike state of consciousness, but when he finally stopped I realized that I was extremely energized and vibrantly experiencing myself and everything around me.

The unique sounds that are made in the transmission of seiki were experienced by Professor Ellen Hemphill, artistic director of Archipelago Theatre at Duke University, voice instructor for the American Dance Festival, and a leading authority on transformative vocalizations. She witnessed the transmission of seiki by both Brad and Osumi and wrote Brad about her thoughts:

I want to thank you again for the experience of meeting you and Mrs. Osumi, and the gift of your extraordinary spirit/energy. . . . I'd also like to comment on the sound that you have tapped into in your work. It is not foreign to me and I have spent 18 years using, teaching, and understanding these "sounds" of the human voice which are, I believe, a passage way into the holy voice, and the healing voice. Holy because used/discovered in the right way, they make us more whole. Healing because when heard on stage the centered voice heals and soothes the listener, and in your work, it is for me clearly a tool for healing the body, in connection with "the laying of hands." Misused or imitated for the sake of imitation, it leads to dis-embodiment and dis-spirited experience. We used to call the moment of inauthentic vocal work "vocal gymnastics," and today there is a lot of that in the art/self-discovery world. Your connection is so genuine and rooted, it is a pleasure and a reward to have been in your "sound waves." Your own experience with the different masters you have worked with has obviously held you to the fire to be true to yourself. Because I am a theatre artist and director, and a voice teacher, and because I work with "truth in art" . . . I have difficulty sometimes to be [sic] clear about the therapeutic moment and the artistic moment. There is never a question about the healing moment. . . . I bristle at psychodrama, or primal scream as mental and self-indulgent and not connected to the creative (versus pathological) aspect of the person. . . . I am sure that the original source of art was the healing rituals—whether healing the body or the spirit—or celebrating life.

Recall how Shakespeare describes the perfect place of dream and sound in this quote from the *Tempest* (Act 3, scene 2).

Be not afeared; the isle is full of noises,
Sounds and sweet airs, that give delight and hurt not.
Sometimes a thousand twangling instruments
Will hum about mine ears; and sometime voices
That, if I then had waked after long sleep,
Will make me sleep again; and then, in dreaming,
The clouds methought would open and show riches
Ready to drop upon me that, when I waked,
I cried to dream again.

Nor Hall, a well-known author, playwright, and Jungian therapist, received seiki from Brad and wrote about her experience with the vital life force.

Keeney lives someplace between *epiphania* and *epidemia*—on the continuum between epiphany and epidemic—where the vibration that "opensings" him becomes contagious. His body acts like a dowsing rod that goes unerringly to the receptive point in another person. It's instinct, or intuition, or an improvisational art based on creating something with whatever elements are put before him.

Keeney's "medicine" is original, unschooled, autonomous, and (often) fast. . . . It appears he doesn't need anything but the instrument of his own body. His body is played: knocked and swayed, sung and spun. Put through the legendary hoops. The energy that moves him in extraordinary ways seems to be readily accessible in ordinary moments. The boundary between states is instantly soluble. I notice also that being in his presence has a way of dissolving the bundling boards that people erect to keep themselves separate. His art/work makes us a tribe. . . .

Keeney weeps easily and laughs easily. When he is fierce, there's a line of graphite that circles the lighter blue of his eyes. This intense and fluctuating expressiveness is also evident in his voice that travels effortlessly from whisper to thunder.

Because of an unselfconscious talent for the mercurial, he shift shapes in response to perceived need. . . . He has no idea what will transpire once the vibration gains momentum. Each encounter generates an original composition.

I meet a continual stream of intelligent people engaged by the psyche. People who are devoted to intelligent soul work and spiritual journeys—and I am among them—but Keeney's radiance shines a different light on the territory. Life happens in dreamtime for him—the soul-in-the-world is alive, and he is, as D. H. Lawrence wrote, in sheer, naked contact with it.

Brad has been giving seiki for several decades now. He has transmitted it in all kinds of situations. Though he has used shamanic tools and spiritual accoutrements from time to time, for the most part he relies only upon a keyboard or his vintage Steinway grand piano to turn our seiki room into an old-fashioned praise house, where song, rhythm, and seiki all fuse together.

Without exception, since our meeting we always work together now when giving seiki. When we are with a client, one of us places our hand on the back of the other, activating the seiki. If Brad is talking, Hillary will send a vibration into his back or hand and activate seiki. Or if Hillary is talking, Brad gives her seiki. Once either of us is flowing with seiki, it becomes contagious and is caught by the other. We recirculate it with each other. There is a reciprocity and collaborative nature to this interaction that makes it impossible to determine who is giving seiki to whom. When one of us demonstrates that seiki is influencing the situation, such as with a dramatic alteration in our voice or movement, it triggers the other to move in kind. Back and forth, we each feed and nurture each other's seiki. When we are sufficiently charged with the vital life force, we are able to share it with our clients.

Even when only one of us is moving or speaking with a client, we are making vibratory contact with one another during this process. This doubles the seiki as it is administered through our relationship and inter-action. We create a kind of seiki triangle where our joined energy can be aimed at a third person. This enhances and empowers the seiki. It also contributes to steering its transmission, for the energy of a two-person interaction—if they are joined—is better than that from a single person. Two merged vibrations are stronger and wiser than a single pulse.

Once when we were hosting a weeklong seiki intensive, the room felt immediately charged with enhanced life force energy from the moment we began. As Hillary put a vibration into Brad's back, he found he could not speak; Brad was so charged that he could only sing.

As he sang with seiki, it lifted the vibrations in Hillary, and she, too, became so filled with seiki that she could only sing. We sang every time we tried to say anything at all. This lasted the entire duration of the intensive, for a full week. The room became the Kalahari, a classical Japanese seiki jutsu clinic, an old-time sanctified revival meeting, a Shakers praise service, and a kundalini cabaret all in one. You can never know when, where, and how seiki will be delivered!

The first time Brad transmitted seiki, it happened spontaneously. Without knowing what he was about to do, he invited a colleague at a university to take a walk with him to the nearby park. They sat down on the grass underneath a palm tree and Brad began vibrating and shaking with seiki. When he passed the vibration into his friend with his hands, they both were shocked to experience what felt like their heads being shot into outer space. Yes, they were launched like a cannon into another experiential dimension. They flew past the stars and witnessed a spectacular light show, accompanied by celestial music that was literally out of this world. When they came back to themselves, they were trembling with joy. In that moment Brad transmitted seiki without knowing what he had done. He realized that he had stumbled upon the greatest secret in the world. Without a doubt he knew this was something beyond words and explanation. It would take him many decades to be ready to teach seiki without holding anything back. With the help of other elders whose cultural traditions were long familiar with the mysteries of the vital life force, Brad was blessed and asked by them to bring seiki to those whose book learning had missed the most important treasure in the world.

Brad experimented with seiki for over forty years in all kinds of venues and situations. He even gave seiki to flight attendants during overnight flights, only telling them he had a way of helping them stay awake. Once he zapped one flight attendant, everyone else got in line. He has given seiki to artists of all kinds, including a series of Soho theatre performers who then brought painters, sculptors, dancers, musicians, poets, and others to receive seiki. They went home having an explosion of creativity that they could not explain.

We have given seiki to drug addicts who after receiving it became bored with drugs and preferred getting high by this natural means. We have also infused Black churches and African American pastors with the spirited enthusiasm their grandparents once knew. The same has happened with Buddhist shamans, including a monk whom Brad was led to in a cave on the Thailand–Burma border; he gave the monk seiki and they danced and shouted with joy. Whether Muslim, Christian, Buddhist, Hindu, shaman, or agnostic scientist, we have transmitted seiki to thousands of people, and although some of them never knew what happened to them, their lives were radically transformed.

Hillary gave her first transmission of seiki to Eduardo, a computer engineer from Campinas, Brazil, who came to see us in the United States. Like Osumi's aunt, without previous warning Brad told Hillary she should give Eduardo seiki. As it had been for Osumi Sensei, Hillary immediately became filled with a sense of confidence and felt the seiki begin to stir inside her. Brad began to play the piano with extraordinary life force, and his music electrified the room. As Eduardo sat on the seiki bench, Hillary's whole body began to vibrate and shake. Her arms swirled in the air, vibratory sounds sprang forth, and her hands began to touch Eduardo's head, back, and shoulders. With the room charged with seiki and filled with ecstatic sounds and soulful music, Hillary felt the seiki boil up inside of her and come forth through her hands into Eduardo like currents of strong, concentrated energy. Eduardo began to rock, sway, and vibrate. Afterward, we all three joyfully celebrated the transmission that had taken place. We also laughed at how Eduardo felt "drunk" on seiki and had to immediately take a three-hour-long nap.

After giving her first seiki transmission, Hillary discovered that now seiki would awaken easily in her, especially when accompanied by Brad's music. Shortly after giving seiki to Eduardo, we conducted a workshop in Toronto, Canada, and it was Hillary who shared seiki with the roomful of participants who lined up to take their turn on the seiki bench while Brad accompanied her on the piano. When we work together this way we feel the seiki current flow between us as if we are one body, and this amplifies the life force in each of us and in the room.

In all his years transmitting seiki, perhaps the most important discovery Brad has made is that it is best administered through the hands of relationship rather than an individual. After many years of involvement with seiki, we became as one being inside it. When this took place, Brad knew that the prophecy many renowned healers and spiritual teachers had spoken to him had come true: Brad had met his other half, his soul mate, and now was the time to bring seiki into the world, doing so with total devotion to its truth, wisdom, and joy.

As a couple who enters seiki together, we follow the way of the Kalahari Bushmen, where relationship rather than individuality holds and transmits the vital life force. The earliest life-force masters always healed inside relationship and community. This is the original way of handling transformation, and this is why we prefer working together with small groups. The future of healing and spiritual teaching will be found in relationship rather than in individual teachers. When we circulate seiki together, we are able to amplify its currents in a stronger way, doing so to such an extent that another person can step into the relational seiki field of energy. Together we all enter the mystery of enhanced seiki. Where there is relationship and community, the life force circulates more freely and is amplified in the circulation.

We find no greater joy than transmitting seiki to others. We have jointly given it to grandparents, students, movie stars, therapists, doctors, teachers, bankers, business professionals, truck drivers, ministers, musicians, and anyone who comes to us wanting to be readied for its reception. If you love God, then seiki will flow. If you love seiki, then God will show up. Call it by any name, but know that an experience of it will never allow you to go back to who you were before. Once you taste it, smell it, see it, hear it, or feel it, your life as you have known it is over. From that moment on, you will be like a Bushman doctor, devoting yourself to the hunt for the life force.

None of us knows how many years we have left in this lifetime. But Brad and I know this: we are devoting every day to helping everyone receive seiki. Get soft so you can experience it. Do so, for nothing else will satisfy the thirst, hunger, and drive that moves you to keep looking for whatever you think will make your life complete. Seiki is the creative life force. It is what inspires creativity and invention. Get yourself 110 percent filled with the force that awakens creativity, the elixir that inspires youth, the tonic that heals physical and emotional wounds, and the holy water that baptizes you in the spiritual mysteries. Seiki has been waiting for you since you were born. Ask for seiki and take one step toward it. The next step will take place spontaneously, without your having to understand anything at all.

Say yes to seiki and then start shouting thank you, for it has been preparing you for its homecoming from the moment you were born.

# 4

# THE DAILY SEIKI
# EXERCISE

The seiki exercise is not merely a practice routine. It would be better if we called it a seiki performance or a seiki flight. When you sit ready to be moved by seiki, it is like being on board a spiritual spacecraft. It can take you into deep inner space or far away into the heights of the visionary cosmos. With this ecstatic portal and mystical means of transport, you are led naturally to the healing, transformative know-how and spiritual gifts you need. Bring your suffering and your joy to this practice and experience seiki transform it all into vital life energy. Everything you bring is the same to seiki—chopped wood to be thrown in its living fire.

Know that the oldest healers and masters of the vital life force have turned to seiki in order to grow their wisdom. Whatever you need to receive can be brought forth when you conduct a seiki performance. At first it will teach you how to let go and be more spontaneous. This, in turn, will activate a new readiness for an enhanced relationship with seiki. Consider your special time with seiki as an opportunity to pull into a spiritual gas station and become filled with life. Also recognize that this is where you will show the gods that you desire the seiki lines and ropes to the holy, wanting to make them more pervasive and evident in your life.

*1.*    You sit and gently press your eyeballs. The motion starts, at first a back and forth rocking, and then a circular motion. All of a sudden energy is stirring at the base of your spine. You start bobbing up and down. Other motions soon join in, all at the same time. Pulses become more complex rhythms that are then embedded inside other rhythmic pulses. All kinds of vibrations can show up on your seiki stage. Allow them to move you. Seiki will tune you inside this extraordinary theatre of effortless movement, what we sometimes call a Life Force Theatre.

Your voice is beginning to make seiki sounds as your hands start patting parts of your body, as if they were dowsing their way to the areas that need attention. Close your eyes and be empty, filled only with seiki. Your mind may begin to fantasize. Give no importance to any thought. Let seiki teach you to discern the fantasies of psychological mind from that which rises from the deeper and more universal spiritual mind. The latter requires no purposeful handling. In seiki your heart is ready to ascend to its rightful place in the symphony of heartfelt callings and longings.

Seiki has made an appointment with you. Simply schedule a time to sit down and introduce yourself. When you learn how to activate the internal switch, you will press "start" and seiki will take over. Once activated, it will be accessible to you forever. The more you nurture seiki, the more it will deliver its gifts. Come experience who you really are. Arrive ready to admit that you know nothing except the fact that you want seiki to lead you to whatever is important, step by step, all along the seiki highway.

Once you are filled with seiki, you need to keep it moving and make it an active participant in your everyday life. Immediately after receiving seiki, it is the traditional Japanese custom to teach the recipient the daily practice of *seiki taisou,* the basic seiki exercise. Here is the miracle: the daily seiki exercise requires no willpower, discipline, or stamina—it consists of three simple steps that are easy to undertake. Unlike aerobic exercise, yoga, diets, and innumerable other therapeutic programs, the daily seiki exercise is effortless.

Some people are reluctant to try out anything new because they recall all the work it took to engage previously with spiritual practices, health strategies, and well-being techniques. What we offer you differs from other things you have tried because it involves *no work*. We are inviting you to take some time for a daily recess where you experience effortless movement. When you master this seiki exercise, endless benefits will enter your life.

Seiki jutsu never asks you to force any movement, thought, attitude, or feeling. It only asks that you take a 10- to 20-minute recess each day to allow yourself to move as your body desires, doing so without purpose, without work, and without effort. In this break from the constant demands of everyday life, life's vital energy will be delivered to you, ready to energetically charge your whole being.

In the traditional Japanese practice of seiki jutsu, you are asked to sit on a wooden stool and then allow your body to perform a spontaneous movement. You simply sit and wait for something to happen. You may sway from side to side or back and forth, bob up and down, or move in circular or elliptical patterns. The movement may be localized more at the base of your spine, in your neck, or in your legs or arms. As you sit on the seiki stool and allow movement, you may fall into any imaginable motion. The pattern may stay locked in one form, or it may change frequently. In seiki jutsu, your body is allowed to play, tinker, and experiment with these motions, and in doing this you learn to fall into movements so natural that you feel as if you are being moved by an unseen force.

*As you slowly lean forward, you also feel a swaying motion beginning to take hold. A tingling energy arrives at your chest and sends a ripple of vibration in your belly that lasts for only a second or two. Now you start to lean back, the swaying amplified and more prominent. As you straighten up on your seiki stool, your arms get hit by a jolt and your elbows suddenly fly outward like wings starting to flap. The energy shoots up your spine, and you bounce on the stool. All these motions seem to be introducing themselves to one another, triggering one another to amplify, modulate, and transform as they interact. From the onset your mind stops its chatter, this performance fully capturing its attention. Every seiki performance is new each time.*

Seiki jutsu reminds you of your earlier expertise in natural movement—when you were a child you allowed your body to move naturally. It happened unconsciously, without any intentional choreography. Now as an adult you are invited to return to those freely expressed movements. Use this freedom of expression to take you into automatic motion, where movement takes place without your having to make it happen. This spontaneous motion can bring you inside the "seiki tuning zone," a place of complete absorption and enhanced awareness. Here you must learn to ride out the motion and feel the ecstatic emotion it brings, allowing seiki to tune you in a natural and effortless way. When you have a sympathetic resonance with the vital life force, it energizes and revitalizes your whole being.

The seiki exercise is both a way to prepare you to receive seiki and a way of nurturing seiki after you have received a transmission. It is not necessary for you to be filled or overflowing with seiki as a prerequisite for initiating the seiki exercise and movements. Anyone at any time can start moving into these effortless rhythms. The spontaneous movements of the seiki exercise help prepare you for receiving seiki, just as the reception of seiki brings forth more enhanced spontaneous movement. When you realize that preparation and reception are not two, but also not one, then you become readied for a life-changing journey with seiki.

Let's get practical and address how seiki can help everyone, even those who are not looking for spiritual transformation. Maybe you simply want to feel more energized in your everyday. Although as a culture we have become fanatical about being healthy and we place a high value on the importance of diet, exercise, and relaxation, many people still struggle with fatigue and stress. Whether standing or sitting, moving or staying still, we get worn out and come face to face with one of the biggest problems of our time: how to get and sustain the energy and vitality to make it through each day.

It's not only the workplace that begs for more vitality. When we go home, we often find that we could use a boost of energy to optimize our time with family and friends. Sometimes the problems and challenges that get us to a therapy session are brought about by simply being worn out from busy or uninspired lives. We lack the energy to deliver what we want to bring to our relationships and instead get cranky and grouchy. This becomes a vicious circle that feeds upon stress, fatigue, and burn out. When we are tired we are susceptible to feeling low. We need some kind of energy boost that can revitalize us to be at our best performance with those we care about the most.

When we think about becoming more creative, imaginative, and spiritually focused in our lives, we may find ourselves lacking the vitality to act beyond our wishful or positive thinking. Too often we don't have the energy to take a stand or to move positively toward our highest goals. Even if our willpower pushes us to become successful, we sometimes find it hard to sustain the energy and inspiration required to go further or even to enjoy the fruits of our efforts. We desperately need more than a coffee break or a moment of relaxation. All of us—men and women, young and old—are looking for a way to easily and quickly recharge ourselves: to give ourselves a true energy break.

We need to renew ourselves with seiki. With seiki, many mysteries can open in your life. The first of these is everyday energy.

By following a simple set of instructions, you will be able to experience and nurture seiki in your daily life. You can shed everyday fatigue, low energy, and lack of vitality for good by working with this simple practice, an exercise that is capable of changing your life forever.

What we have to teach about the seiki energy exercise requires no complicated understanding, special initiation, or indoctrination. It is a simple, natural, and effortless practice that you can begin right this very moment. As you will discover, you have held this know-how inside of you for your whole life, but it has been hidden or forgotten. Our job is to lead you back to the most remarkable resource that was ever given to you.

The goal of the seiki exercise is to get you in tune. You know you are out of tune if you spend a lot of time worrying or analyzing, whether it is about problems of the past or imagined difficulties of the future. You might experience this worry as a pain in your gut, a stiffness in your back or neck, or a tightness in your chest. Or you may not sleep well at night. You also are out of tune whenever you experience a sense of dread with regard to your everyday responsibilities, including upcoming tasks, activities, or meetings. It is possible to get so out of tune that you physically bump into things throughout the day; your body feels off balance, and you find it difficult to concentrate and focus on what you are doing; your mind wanders or things easily irritate you.

When there's little excitement or enthusiasm in your daily life, you are out of tune. When you find yourself predicting the worst, that you will be dealt with unfairly, or you find yourself always missing victory, then you are out of tune. Perhaps you wonder whether there is something wrong with your body or whether you need to see a therapist. Life seems like an obstacle course, and you find yourself becoming more cynical. You have less zeal and idealism than you did when you were younger, and you find yourself easily caught up in petty interactions. Everything feels off course, and you've lost your compass. Though you talk about spirituality, your life lacks spirit; the only mystery left for you is why anyone could possibly be mystified by anything. The magic has slipped away. You have lost your mojo. You wish you could have enough energy and vitality to try anything new just one more time. This is what it is to be out of tune.

When you are in tune, your body movements feel natural. You have a natural grace and rhythm in your motion, and at times you feel as though you are being lifted off the ground. Instead of worry you feel joy, excitement, and enthusiasm about life. There is electricity in the air, and most moments are filled with hope and eager anticipation. Your body often tingles with excitement. You are focused and immersed in whatever you are doing and have a true passion for things. Being tuned enables you to be so absorbed in the moment that you have little concern for past or future. When properly tuned you become comfortably tired and are able to enjoy a well-deserved rest. Life feels natural, and it takes little to no effort to feel "on" and to believe in yourself. Others see you filled with energy, vitality, and charisma. You revitalize others when they are around you. It is difficult for you to get inappropriately irritated, for you see all of life's ups and downs as part of the wholeness of life's richness. When tuned, you celebrate other people's joy and enjoy sharing your life with them. Instead of talking about spirituality you walk it, as you are less interested in discussing dreams than living them. A tuned life abounds with mystery. Every day holds wonder and enchantment. These experiences mark the tuned life.

The seiki exercise is a practice that aims to tune you so you can enter this way of being. As your relationship to seiki grows, even when the winds of life blow you out of tune, you find it much easier to (literally) wiggle your way back into alignment. Here life begins to happen naturally, without much effort, and sometimes the movement of your life is so smooth that you feel like you are just going along for the ride. Like a river that flows naturally down its banks, your life moves without any resistance or interruption. This effortless living is the surest sign that the life force is with you.

It is time for you to learn how to tune yourself with the seiki exercise and discover how to awaken the first mystery of receiving a boost of vital energy. As you continue nurturing seiki through this practice, other mysteries are ready to make themselves available to you. As you will soon discover, the secret of seiki involves moving your body in resonance with the pulse of life itself.

## THE THREE STEPS OF THE SEIKI EXERCISE

Like learning to ride a bicycle, once you get the hang of this exercise and its movement, it will naturally fall into place and happen on its own. Once you feel the natural motion your body is designed to perform, you won't be able to live without it. There won't be a single day that goes by without tapping into seiki in this way.

When we look past particular spiritual beliefs and historic customs, we find that the world's most powerful spiritual and healing practices get you in tune with the vital life force. The easiest way to activate this tuning process is to get your body pulsing, creating a kind of positive resonance that brings seiki into you.

With the three steps outlined below, we have identified the essence of the seiki practice, pairing it down to its basic principles so that it may be easily learned and practiced by anyone. The seiki exercise basically involves these three sequential steps.

**Step One—Initiate a body movement that has rhythm.** From sitting, start a simple motion of your body, such as rocking, that turns into a vibrant rhythmic pulse.

**Step Two—Continue improvising a moving perforn**
Exprcss somc improviscd body movcmcnt, ranging from small movements to dance-like gestures, and feel free to make sounds.

**Step Three—Enter the seiki tuning zone.** Allow the free and spontaneous expression of your body to carry you into an ecstatic awareness that is free of mind-body dualisms and disassociated experience. We playfully refer to this as the "seiki tuning zone."

Let's look at each of these steps in a bit more depth now.

## Step One

### *Initiate a Body Movement That Has Rhythm*

Find yourself a bench, stool, or chair for this practice. The Japanese tradition of seiki jutsu uses a wooden bench that is seventeen inches high, with a seat measuring sixteen by nine inches. It doesn't matter what kind of chair you use as long as you are able to move easily while sitting on it. You definitely do not want to sit in a chair that you readily sink or fall back into. A flat surface is best; soft, thick cushions or upholstery should be avoided. We do not suggest using meditation cushions, as they can restrict movement of the feet and legs.

When you sit down to start the exercise, close your eyes and take a moment to transition into the first step. Press the inner corner of each eyeball with the middle or second finger of each hand, doing so gently. This sends a signal to your autonomic nervous system that you are beginning the practice of seiki jutsu.

Now begin a rocking motion of your body. At the start of your seiki practice you can do anything you want to get this movement going, including faking it. Don't worry whether you are making the right motion or not. *In this practice there are no wrong movements.* Just start moving to get things started. Wiggle, rock, fidget, or raise your arms— do whatever comes to you. At first you are simply getting a motion started that will hopefully trigger an automatic movement, which will appear without any conscious effort on your part. As you begin moving,

*Einstein* consider this wisdom teaching from Albert Einstein: "Nothing happens until something moves." What he did not say is equally true: "Nothing moves until something happens."

Do anything to get yourself moving. Imagine that you are allowing some wound-up tension to be released. Watch your body begin to literally unwind through rocking, vibrating, and coiling motions. Or imagine that you are handing yourself over to seiki and that if you wiggle a bit in order to be noticed, seiki will eventually grab hold and move you. Try swaying with the wind, languidly moving your body like a cat or dog does during a yawn, or rocking in a way that helps free you from the controlling grip of your conscious mind. You may also sit down on your practice seat and simply wait for the rhythm to come forth, like the early Quakers used to patiently wait for the spirit to show up and move them. If you are not sure how to get started, then a rocking chair may be the best place for you to begin. Use a chair that is easy to rock in. Do your seiki exercise there, experimenting with various rocking motions until you are able to fall into a movement that seems to be taking place on its own. It will feel like the chair is rocking itself and that you have nothing to do with the movement. As simple as this method may seem, this is one of the most powerful means of learning to initiate an automatic movement. When you become skilled at triggering this automatic rocking, move from the rocking chair to another chair and allow the same automatic rocking to arise.

You can also purchase or make yourself a pendulum with a string or thread that holds a tiny weight. Hold in it your hand and allow the swinging to take place until it really feels like it is happening on its own. Know that the moving pendulum is actually the unconscious spontaneous motion of your body. Imagine transferring what you see with the string into your body as you sit on the bench. Allow yourself to become a pendulum so that your spine moves as if someone is suspending you with a string from above.

Another helpful trigger is thinking about that which inspires you most: your spiritual beliefs, your philosophy of life, someone you love, joyful memories, exalting music, a thrilling scene in a film. Think of those things that excite you and lift your spirit. As your emotions are awakened, allow your body to tremble, wiggle, or move with excitement; such a jolt of body excitement can be used to start your motion machine. Keep priming yourself with exciting thoughts and emotions until the motions start coming forth.

In the beginning it may take a couple of minutes, or longer, for you to get an appropriate motion started. As you become more familiar with how to get things going, though, this first step will take less than a minute, and it may require only a few seconds for you to get the spontaneous motions launched.

The transition from forced body movements to a natural and spontaneous rhythmical pulse is the key moment in the seiki practice.

Once you've had an experience or two with feeling your body move naturally, you will learn how to let go into such movement with little effort and wait time. But in the beginning, you may have to explore various ways of awakening this motion and getting yourself jump started. You are already wired to have this experience in your daily life. You now have to find a way to turn it on. Once you find the start button, all you have to do is push it.

The first step is the most important one in your beginning work with seiki, and you should take as much time as necessary for you to get a vibrant rhythm going. One of the benefits of starting your experience of seiki with a seiki jutsu master is that a master is able to move you physically so you can experience automatic movement without any effort. This is one of the benefits of having someone familiar with seiki help get you on track. But you can come to know natural movement and learn how to drop into it with this kind of practice. Be patient with your learning. Once your body is familiar with doing this, it will take place almost automatically.

In his classic book, *Zen and the Art of Archery,* Eugen Herrigel writes about his time in Japan where he learned the art of archery from a Zen perspective. Over and over his master would teach: "The right art is purposeless, aimless! The more obstinately you try to learn how to shoot the arrow for the sake of hitting the goal, the less you will succeed in the one and the further the other will recede."[1] Similarly, the more you try to force a natural rhythm, the further from success you will likely drift. The challenge is to tinker with as many movements as you can and then wait patiently.

The patience of waiting for the accident that trips you into a natural rhythm is poetically described by Herrigel's teacher: "It is all so simple. You can learn from an ordinary bamboo leaf what ought to happen. It bends lower and lower under the weight of snow. Suddenly the snow slips to the ground without the leaf having stirred."[2]

There is something more complex going on than a spark of conscious will that triggers an action. As you find yourself falling into natural pulses and rhythms, you will find that the release of seiki comes of its own accord, without being forced. You discover that you have stopped swimming against the current. No longer does movement feel forced. You become as flexible as a bamboo leaf that yields to the weight of snow or the movement of wind, not because you are passive, but because you've become free, loose, and springy, able to be moved by unexplainable and indescribable natural currents.

*Seiki arrives without notice. It's here in an instant, showing up the moment you forget about trying to receive it, as you feel absorbed in the movements. There is no longer mind or body. The more they disappear, the more you become seiki. Forget being an empty cup. Be less. Jump into the stream, not to be carried away, but to become the water. Then become less than the stream. Only the movement. In the changing is found the rearranging, the exchanging everything for changing.*

## Step Two

### *Continue Improvising a Moving Performance*

When your actions are effortless and you find yourself surprised by the ease at which they come forth, you will find that you have truly entered a more spontaneous way of being in the exercise. In this flow experience, you are *improvising;* that is, making up your own movements as you go along, as opposed to rigidly following a preformed strategy of action.

Ken Werner, a premier jazz pianist, gave a speech at the International Association of Jazz Educators in 1991 in which he described his experience of improvising: "The music is there already before you play it. . . . All you have to do is tap into it and it's going to flow out at such an alarming rate that the task will be to stop it, to shut it off, so you can go to sleep after the gig." This is the essence of pure improvisation. It is jumping onto a wave of the creative life force that then expresses itself through you, rather than you forcing anything to happen.

Once you have been caught by a spontaneous rhythmic pulse in a seiki exercise, recognize that this is the opening to the flow of improvised expression. Allow the energy to express itself as it calls you to do so. You can make dance-like movements or feel free not to do so. Your voice can be used to make sounds, whether they are musical or not. You may whistle like a bird, growl like a lion, sing operatic notes, or sing scat to invented melodies. Rather than discerning right and wrong action, explore what feels like natural, authentic expression. Oscar Peterson, the prodigious jazz pianist, once commented that in jazz there is no such thing as a "wrong note."[3] There are only outcomes that can be woven into the flow of an ongoing sequence of notes. If a jazz musician hits an unexpected note, then he can celebrate the surprise and use it to take him in an unanticipated direction. Every note is accepted as contributing to the ongoing creative flow. Furthermore, as any music lover can tell you, listening to someone play all the right notes without heart and soul can be dreadfully boring, whereas playing a wrong note with heart and soul is musically and aesthetically "right."

If you make what you think are right movements, but they don't feel effortless and authentic, then they are not natural. However, if you make movements that you can't imagine being right—because they are odd, too small, or without meaning—but they feel effortless, then you are right on. Allow whatever is flowing to flow.

When you do not feel an authentic flow of movement, or if you lose the rhythm, don't worry about it. Wait it out, return to step one, and start again. Your seiki exercise will have its own rhythms, going in and out of the rhythmic flow, and this will happen more on some days than others. Respect and even cherish the moments when you are out of the flow, because those are the opportunities for you to experiment with new ways of getting back in the groove.

With step two, you move a step closer to getting tuned by seiki. Here you learn firsthand that seiki and the creative force are the same. Tapping into your creative energy is nothing less than hitting the main line of seiki, the vital life force. This helps explain why a complete immersion in a creative project is so rejuvenating.

In step one, you go into motion in order to catch a natural pulse and rhythm. Once this rhythmic pulse is established, your body commences step two, the free-form improvisation of movement and sound. Step two is the final preparation for moving you into the seiki tuning zone, the place where you become charged with the life force.

*It only takes a second or two for you to be grabbed by an automatic motion. As you enter the rhythmic pulse, you feel a newborn confidence and joy. The joy of being alive inspires you to say "Thank you." There you are in your seiki performance, shouting and singing "Thank you." As you move, the seiki river rises. It begins to heat up and boil. Then you feel a pulsing, an inner rhythm like the chugging of a steam engine. It rises up and out of your voice. The steam starts to cook you from the inside out, making your insides shine. Seiki has come to replace psychology. No longer are you concerned about self-esteem. This show is all about making*

*spiritual steam, taking all the junk and all the glory of life, turn-ing it into a holy vapor and releasing it out of the top of your head.*

*Enter the seiki dream where all is improvised. Hit a wrong note and then make it right by how it is freed to encourage a different kind of flight. You are improvising, jamming, no longer hindered by whatever you thought was blocking the way. Enter the flow that brings a glow and takes what's stuck and lets it go. "Thank you." You thank rather than think.*

### Step Three

### *Enter the Seiki Tuning Zone*

When you are captured by a spontaneous rhythmic pulse and it inspires improvisational expression, you become like a surfer catching a wave. In surfing you wait for a wave to come along, then you attempt to catch it and be carried on an exhilarating ride. Similarly, the movement you aim to bring forth in the first two steps of the seiki exercise is analogous to waiting for a wave or current. First you catch a rhythmic pulse, and then you ride its improvisational expression.

This ride carries you to step three, the seiki tuning zone. Here you become less conscious of what you are doing and feel completely absorbed in an experience that hosts a transformative kind of height-ened awareness. However, if you become too excited by what's happen-ing and start gloating over it, you will disconnect yourself from the tuning zone. Similarly, if you start analyzing or worrying about whether it will last, you will get derailed. Your whole being must stay dissolved in (rather than focused on) the experience at hand and not drift into commentary, reflection, or ego fantasy. Stay grounded in the experience, and do not permit your mind to float away like a cartoon bubble that fills with commentary.

We are speaking of pure absorption in immediate here-and-now experience. The seiki exercise orients you toward this absorption experi-ence in which you resonate with the pulse of that which is pulsing—the immediate life you are presently in. This tuning zone is where your life becomes completely in synch, in the groove, on track, and in tune with the spontaneous flow of life.

#1    When you fall into the rhythmic pulse of step one, you feel the beginning of a change in how you experience what is going on around you. #2 When the motion grabs you in step two and moves you to be more improvisational, it brings you an expanded awareness of present possibilities. All this happens without any effort on your part. You enter step three when #3 you are fully absorbed in the experience, as all parts of you unite into being a unitary whole. Here wholeness heals, guides, and tunes. This is the seiki tuning zone. Without any effort, you are able to enter realms that other spiritual practices take years or a lifetime to achieve. Here the practice is the end, rather than a means to an end. Or to say it differently, there is no end and no means; only a moving beginning. Beginner's mind asks for beginner's body, both required for beginning a new life.

Seiki jutsu teaches you to ride the natural flow of life. It doesn't take that long to have a transformative ride with seiki. Only a few minutes—sometimes two, or five, ten minutes, or longer if you want—will be enough to get tuned. Give yourself at least ten minutes interspersed here and there throughout the day in order to benefit from being exercised by seiki. As you make more room for this experience, it will grow and its effects will gradually become more immediate and powerful. Over the years, you will find that these seiki performances become an automatic part of your life, so that seiki itself starts performing you whenever it desires.

Each time you make time to call forth a seiki performance, you will notice that it naturally comes to a close. As you feel your consciousness moving away from the movements and more toward everyday life, allow your movements to slow down and finally come to a stop. When the movement ceases, gently press your fingers to the inner corners of your eyes again, as you did in the beginning. This time a message is sent that the seiki performance has ended. You will come out feeling ready to start life all over again.

When you begin performing with seiki, we suggest that you schedule it at least once a day. Start with small sessions, and don't overdo it.
It is better for you to start with an effortless one-minute performance
than force yourself to go through a lot of hard work. If it feels like a
drag, then you are not connected with seiki.

As you move more easily into this life force performance theatre,
allow its expression to evolve at its own rate. You will eventually begin
adding more time for seiki as you feel more desire for it. Some performances may only last a minute or two, whereas others may last longer. Twenty minutes is considered a good session. As you become more
experienced with being moved by seiki, it will become as vital to your
well-being as sleep and good food. You will learn to appreciate the variety of ways you can infuse seiki movements into your daily activities.
You do not always have to go through all three steps as we have defined
them. The steps may eventually become one single step in which getting
a rhythmic pulse, moving improvisationally, and going into the seiki
tuning zone all happen at the same time. You may find that you can
initiate a tiny movement or vibration that is not perceptible to anyone,
and then proceed to tune yourself to be more effective in an ongoing
public interaction. This is already done by business executives in Japan
who have been taught seiki jutsu.

The seiki exercise provides you with more than a once-a-day practice that you can add to your life. It is a way of hooking up to energy,
vitality, and inspiration that can be used at any moment. Though you
will learn more about seiki as you regularly move with it, know that
this will eventually lead to a time when you can do it under any circumstances and in any situation. You will find that whenever you need
a boost of seiki, all you have to do is bring forth a particular vibration
into your body and allow it to carry you into the tuning zone.

*We know you can have a wonderful and prosperous relationship*
*with seiki. After introducing yourself to it as a daily exercise,*

*proceed to exorcise the word "exercise." Perhaps you need to make yourself a personal theatre ticket that provides lifetime admission to your Life Force Theatre. Schedule a show every day and don't miss a performance. Do it as if your life force depends on it.*

*A day will come when you find what every master of the life force has as her most cherished possession. You will discover that you own seiki, which is to say that seiki owns you. By this we mean you own the feeling for it, have a relationship with it, a line of connection with it that can never be broken. In the beginning, you schedule your performances. This helps prepare you for the future when seiki takes over and starts scheduling its performances with you.*

*When this happens you will find that a high-frequency vibration will spontaneously enter your head whenever you need revitalization, healing, guidance, or spiritual instruction. An inner voice will direct you, visionary guidance will appear, and your body will acquire a new dictionary regarding what is felt in the world. This entry into a relationship with seiki brings you together as one. What you feel in a great performance now remains inside of you. Your whole life becomes a Life Force Theatre and you are never off stage. There you are performed by seiki.*

Sept. 22-2014

Seiki gives you an edge in all the activities of your life. As you learn to tune yourself throughout the day, your physical well-being will light up, enabling you to have a healthy glow. Your attitude and outlook will change, and you will become filled with a certainty that you can do all the important things you desire accomplishing. There is no better health supplement, success technique, or spiritual teacher than having regular contact with seiki.

As you become more familiar with falling into seiki movement, you will invent your own modifications that improve its effectiveness for you. Every way is right as long as it brings you into natural, effortless motions that circulate and enhance seiki. With seiki, you always begin at the final lesson—learning to be spontaneously natural. You do not have to wait years learning what you will eventually have to throw away in the future. You begin where you want to end, and then, with each passing month and year, you move more deeply into the original mysteries of ecstatic living. Here the art of the body's effortless motion, the mind's spontaneous flow, and the soulful expression of the creative spirit all move together. Seiki makes you whole and opens the door to all that is holy.

*You are like a rocket sitting on the launch pad. The engines are rumbling as energy builds up at the base of your spine. You can hear and feel the pulse of its countdown: "5, 4, 3, 2, 1, liftoff!" A powerful bolt of energy rises up your spine. Seiki becomes your pilot. Soon you feel no gravity. Your body feels weightless and able to perform movements it couldn't do under usual conditions. Close your eyes and feel the purest joy imaginable. Seiki can take you anywhere.*

*Seiki took Osumi Sensei inside her own body, where she received her anatomy lessons. She traveled through all her internal structures and organs. Years later she became a research assistant to a professor of anatomy at a medical school in Tokyo. She was happy to see that seiki had taught her well. Seiki will bring you a teaching—some know-how, personal guidance, special direction—and a gift whenever it is time for you to receive it. Get ready by allowing seiki to move you. When you are ready, seiki will move you, change and transform you. It is the original transformation, the source of all spiritual mysteries.*

*What changes as you get deeper into seiki? As you become one with seiki, you find that mind serves seiki rather than creating the delusion that you were ever separate from it. You find that an absorption experience is nothing less than being dissolved in seiki. Now things are aligned and in synch. Everything comes together, including all the rhythms of your body, from ultradian to circadian, as well as micro and macro rhythms, cultural tides, mythological waves, and the vibrating music of the spheres. In the heart of seiki is found the most beautiful music. Seiki is the voice, rhythm, tone, and harmonics of holiness. It is the first movement of creation and the ultimate rhythm of all that is.*

There was an amazing music teacher in Boston named Madame Chaloff who taught famous pianists, including Keith Jarrett and Herbie Hancock. She began with a simple lesson on playing one note effortlessly and perfectly. Once you learned that lesson, all else would follow. In other words, all you need to learn is how to be authentically spontaneous for one moment; the rest is detail. Stop practicing in order to get good enough to be able to do it. Start performing. Do not have a seiki practice, and do not engage in a seiki exercise. Perform seiki to learn that seiki wants to perform you. There is nothing else to be said about this; anything else is commentary on this one truth.

The American healer Agnes Sanford, author of *The Healing Light,* encouraged people to enter into energy work with a prayer. For those with religious faith, she would say something like, "Heavenly Father, please increase in me your life-giving power." For those who weren't comfortable with religious talk, she would advise a prayer such as, "Whoever you are, whatever you are, come into me now." It is wise to add, "Thy will be done," or to say it in the terms in which we're exploring now: "May seiki, the vitality of life, be in charge." This request moves you into a sacred relationship with life's greater wisdom and attunes you to be more in synch with its pulse and movement.

While the vibrations of seiki will come without prayer, adding prayer gives you a supercharge. If you enter into it with a voice that hands yourself to the whole of life, your performance will be naturally enhanced.

Osumi Sensei would always offer a prayer before giving someone seiki, asking that seiki bring them great joy and happiness. We ask the same for you. We are mindful of these words from Lao Tzu: "He who is in harmony with the Tao is like a newborn child." It is time for you to receive seiki, letting "all things come and go effortlessly." May seiki bring you great joy and happiness.

# 5

# THE ENERGIZED BODY

## Using Spontaneous Movement to Heal

The ancestral spirits speak in dream time:

Healer, you must first administer medicinal vibrations. Know that any other form of medicine is secondary. An attuned vibration must activate the body's natural ability to absorb whatever else is given.

The same is true for dispensing prayer. To be blessed, the body must be vibrating to receive the sacred resonance of uttered holy sound.

This also holds for the biggest love. The heart must flutter in order to move the wings of ecstatic flight.

And so it is for everything from the handling of suffering to being blessed by grace. With vibration we are able to be more fully caught by all that life offers.

Healer, first tremble yourself. Then pass the vibration to others. This is how spiritual medicine is delivered.

Spontaneous movement is a natural part of maintaining life. It is one of the ways you automatically regulate your body functions. For instance, heartbeat, breathing, yawning, peristalsis of the digestive organs, and blinking of the eyelids are involuntary spontaneous movements that are always taking place in your body.

Healers from all over the world have known that, in addition to involuntary movements, it is possible to induce spontaneous movements—especially vibrations that activate the body's natural abilities to heal. Some contemporary bodyworkers report new discoveries that spontaneous movements, including trembling and shaking, can help heal trauma, injury, and disease. In reality, this is actually one of the oldest teachings of cultural healing traditions throughout the world.

While vibration is associated with the healing response, what has often gone without recognition is the fact that the vibrations of a healer can help activate healing vibrations in the client. The bodyworker, healer, or movement coach must be tuned to catch the rhythmic pulse that can help others have a vibration that gets natural healing in motion. When you see people teaching about life force energy and claiming to conduct energy healing, pay less attention to how they explain it. It doesn't matter whether one talks about healing or energy in terms of quantum theory, spirituality, or vibrational medicine. What matters is whether you notice a vibration in the healer. Does that person move as if he or she is plugged into an unseen electrical source? Do they touch others with vibrating hands, or are their hands, voice, and body motions lifeless, lacking the vitality of the non-subtle life force? If people are passing out in the aisles and there is no visible vibration in the healer's hands, body, and voice, then you are most likely witnessing group hypnosis and suggestive influence. This is equally true for both religious and New Age congregations. Be forewarned: there is an enormous amount of misinformation taking place in the name of the vital life force and healing.

Seiki is obvious. You see it, hear it, and feel it. As the old Bushman healers say, you can even smell and taste it. There is nothing phony or false about seiki and there is no need for quasi-scientific metaphors to convince you that it is real. With seiki, words are not primarily used to persuade. They are used to celebrate and give praise for the bliss and the immediacy that the non-subtle vital life force delivers. If someone is authentically trembling, shouting, and singing with joy, then he has seiki. Get as close to this seiki as you can. Everything inside of you is vibrating, including the billions of body cells that pulse in different frequencies. Healthy cells have a different frequency of vibration than unhealthy cells in diseased areas of the body. The key to activating spontaneous recovery is found in how you change vibrations; when these vibrations are changed, you create a favorable climate for healing. When a healer is vibrating with vitality and health, that frequency can be passed on to another person. No need to think of this as bodywork, physical medicine, or healing. It's simply bringing someone inside a dance with seiki. If you are vibrating with the vital life force, then dance with someone. Hold their hands, lift their arms, and move them in all the spontaneous ways that seiki inspires.

*Have you heard about the dance studio that teaches you how to dance with the vital life force? Inside we find a different kind of instructor, one who helps people be danced by seiki. The setting looks like a classic dance studio with a grand piano; someone is playing music as movement is performed. There is the instructor, lifting one arm and tilting her head as another dance begins. Now she's dancing with someone who is sitting in a chair. Shaking and swaying like a tree in the wind, she helps you catch the rhythm that moves your life.*

The earth vibrates at approximately 7.83 cycles per second. This is the measurement of the magnetic wave frequencies that pulse between the earth's surface and the ionosphere, the part of the atmosphere that begins about twenty-five miles above the earth. Scientists refer to this rhythm as the Schumann resonance, and it has been proposed that it is the pulse or heartbeat of Earth itself.

Our bodies are able to move with this very same rhythm. Zen masters produce an alpha brain wave during meditation that pulses at 7.83 beats per second. The fluttering hands of ecstatic healers also move at this frequency. We can ask whether falling into the same beat as the universal life force enables a sympathetic flow of energy from the ocean of energy that surrounds us, enabling it to pour directly into the body. Move yourself into the 7.83 vibration, doing so with everything from body trembling to brain wave activity. When you fall into this rhythm, you create the conditions to be tuned and healed as energy naturally flows through you.

*Do you remember what your high school or college science teacher taught about sympathetic resonance? If you place two tuned violins in two different corners of a room and only play one violin's string, the other violin's string will vibrate and make the same sound. If you and I are tuned instruments, then playing one of us transmits or sets up a sympathetic resonance with the other, so both of us are played. Seiki works with this principle. Hold on to a seiki master, and as seiki tunes him, you will be tuned. When seiki plays either of you, both of you are played.*

There is nothing to teach about how to use seiki for healing other than reminding you to go to school with seiki. Osumi Sensei learned at the seiki stool and so can you. Whether it is transmitting seiki, helping make someone soft enough for reception, or administering it in a therapeutic way to facilitate healing (what Osumi Sensei called *seiki-ryouhou*), there is no routine, model, or protocol that can be followed. You simply have to get enough seiki in you and allow it to lead you to spontaneously perform. The latter point cannot be stressed enough: it is not technique that makes a healer, but the degree to which that person is herself plugged in to the vital life force when interacting with another.

When you are filled with seiki, you are automatically led to the "treatment points," as Osumi Sensei called them. These are the areas on the body that are ready to receive seiki. Their locations vary according to the present condition of the client's body, the geographical location and weather, and how many seiki treatments have already been received, among other factors. Treatment points do not occupy fixed positions within a rigidly defined system. Instead, they are constantly changing in relation to the particular needs of each unique individual.

If you are a bodyworker, you may have learned specific procedures for working with clients. All this may have been useful in the beginning of your training to help alleviate your anxiety about what to do with a client, but later this gets in the way and becomes too restrictive. Having worked with master healers and bodyworkers all over the world, we have found that they all share one thing in common—they are master improvisors. Though their explanations may vary, when it comes down to working with a client they do not follow any specific healing protocol or model. Instead, they work as the client's body calls them to perform. This is the sign of an authentic, well-developed healer.

We have given seiki to many bodyworkers and have helped free them from any and all practice models that restrict their improvisational presence with a client. In addition to awakening the healing gifts of a bodyworker, seiki jutsu brings forth healing skills for all practitioners. As you work with seiki in your daily performance exercise, you will find that a time will come when a natural healing response spontaneously comes forth. Your hands will start treating yourself as they touch, rub, poke, pat, tap, and vibrate various parts of your body. You will find the desire to touch those close to you, especially your family members. We encourage this exploration of seiki touch with a loved one.

One of the strongest contexts for holding the life force and administering it to others is found among the Kalahari Bushmen, who conduct most of their healing in community dances. Here, no touching interaction is framed as "bodywork." It is instead regarded as a part of the healing dance. Imagine dance halls with live bands where people not only dance for fun or courtship, but for healing as well. That's what you find in the Kalahari—outdoor sandlot dance grounds where people dance with seiki. Here healing, inspiration, and guidance spontaneously appear without having to be named as anything other than the arrival and movement of seiki.

In religious ceremonies of laying on of hands, the hands do not have to be still, nor does the person receiving the touch. If you are actually feeling the holy spirit, your hands definitely will be trembling. What gets passed from one person to another is a vibration, and this is the carrier wave of seiki. When the vibration is transferred, new frequencies are activated within the recipient, opening all kinds of experiential possibilities. Though healers have many different metaphors and understandings of what is taking place—depending upon the cultural tradition in which they were brought up—they share a recognition that spiritual presence is marked by spontaneous body movements.

Masters of the non-subtle life force don't distinguish between moments when they are healing someone, preparing another for receiving the life force, or giving it. Instead, they are often moved by something sacred and holy that leads to a spontaneous handling and sharing of the vital life force. They are instruments available for a higher power to act through them. Though it may be tempting to ignore healers' spiritual beliefs and reduce their work to a core practice or technique, a healer's relationship to spirituality may be what is most responsible for attracting and amplifying the life force. It is next to impossible to reach the highest frequencies and most transformative vibrations without a profound love of holiness and respect for that which is its source.

*They may call you a healer, but all you feel is gratitude for the joy that is circulating inside of you. Others may call it the life force, but you know it's the holiness of life, a gift from God. When it*

*circulates inside, all things are possible, though always outside your will. You are only an instrument for expressing creation's never-ending movement. Jump into the heart of God's love. It is guaranteed to move you. When someone comes asking for help, just say, "All aboard! This ship is bound for glory." That's what you are—a ship on holy water. Hold that person's hand and he will be touched by what touches you. Never mind what it is or how to talk about it, let alone explain it—just feel it move you. The only words worth saying are "thank you."*

Those who love God—who feel a big love for divinity—will likely have more seiki than those who believe that quantum theory or core techniques are all the metaphors needed to deliver its efficacy. We are not inviting a head trip about belief, whether it professes religious wisdom, spiritual principles, or New Age platitudes. We are referring to an experienced relationship with holiness, whose intimate contact makes you tremble and voice a sound of praise. This, more than anything, marks a master of the vital life force.

If you feel no need or desire to be a professional bodyworker, but feel called to work with seiki movements, then consider becoming a coach of spontaneous, seiki-filled body jazz. Make certain that you differentiate yourself from ecstatic dancing, which sometimes loses an awareness of seiki and gets caught in presumed assumptions about dance. Ecstatic, improvisational dance or "shaking" gatherings may or may not have any relationship to seiki. It is seiki, not just the wild movement of the body, that carries us into ecstatic experience.

*Let's put on some George Gershwin, Cole Porter, or whatever music stirs your feelings. Imagine dressing up your fingers in miniature formal dance wear. Put some tiny dancing shoes on the tips*

*of each finger. Draw them if you like. Now ask your significant
other to lie down so her back becomes your dance floor. Then say
to your partner, "Let's dance." Let those fingers dance, glide, and
jump across your tactile floor.*

We ask our clients to sit on a Japanese seiki stool in front of us. We
may hold one or both of their hands as we make contact with seiki.
Usually our eyes are closed as our voice changes, now empowered with
the non-subtle life force. As we move, our clients move with us. Or
Hillary may talk or sing as Brad stands to administer a spirited vibration to a client's neck or head. In seiki body therapeutics, spontaneous
movements come forth when the client's body calls out for transformative vibrations. They unconsciously ask for a dance with seiki.

Some of our students and clients are dancers. Whether they know
it or not, all dancers are hunting for seiki. As an accomplished dancer
herself, Hillary has found that seiki is the key to inspiring any form of
dance, from free-form improvisation to more constrained forms such as
tango, salsa, flamenco, or swing. All dancers seek those rare moments
when movement becomes effortless and it feels as if the dance is dancing the dancer. The latter, what flamenco dancers call "duende," is made
more possible when seiki is present,

We once had a session with a teacher of ecstatic dance from Santiago,
Chile. Although her dance was improvisational, she complained that
her movements had begun to feel habituated and contrived. As she
described it, with tears in her eyes, "Although I move freely and have
had moments of ecstasy, I have never truly fallen into the seiki stream.
I long to be danced by seiki." Hillary asked if she ever tried dancing
tango. Sometimes, when improvisation becomes too purposeful, the
constraints of form and partner paradoxically bring us more deeply into
relationship to spontaneous movement. The woman responded, "I have
tried it, but I do not like to dance with a partner because then I do not
feel free." Without a word, Hillary got up and put on some slow tango

music, then took the woman's hand and led her to the center of the room. As the audience watched, Hillary took the woman in her arms in a tango-like embrace and began to dance her with seiki. At first the woman's body was stiff, but soon she relaxed and allowed her body to be moved. Seiki proceeded to dance both dancers and the atmosphere of the room became charged with electrical-like energy. The experience was so strong that the woman and members of the audience began to weep. Together they fell into a seiki dance, when two bodies become one, danced by something greater than any sum.

*We are feeling something now. We are feeling it this very moment, as seiki pulses and marks its own time and way with us. We are happy that seiki is here, moving us. This is a time when transformations can happen, so let's open our hearts and let the movements have their say—wherever they take us is where we'll go, making ourselves available for holiness to bless any mess, and happy to know that it is time to go deeper into what really matters.*

Brad was once asked by a board member of Dr. John Upledger's institute in Palm Beach, Florida, to show up for a surprise visit with Dr. Upledger, a founder of cranial-sacral therapy. Brad's visit was Dr. Upledger's birthday present, given by some of those who were close to him. Brad and John had met before and discovered that they each were passionate fans of the jazz pianist Erroll Garner. Both men played jazz piano and spent the evening performing for each other. Brad then gave a demonstration of seiki to Dr. Upledger. He was so excited about its direct and non-subtle quality that he formally endorsed seiki jutsu as "going straight to the core of healing . . . an energy practice anyone can learn and benefit from." Brad hung out with Dr. Upledger for a week; they visited patients all day and took turns giving each other treatments.

They discussed the need for a "people's movement" that would be like the barefoot doctors of China, enabling the healing practices of practical energy work like seiki jutsu to be in the hands of all people, not just professionals. Brad told Dr. Upledger how this had happened in Japan during the early twentieth century, when a popular health movement spread through the country, teaching seiki jutsu to everyone.

We have now trained medical doctors, surgeons, dermatologists, pediatricians, internists, radiologists, osteopaths, chiropractors, Alexander practitioners, Rolfers, reiki practitioners, nurses, and many other "people-helpers" how to use seiki in their professional practice. One of our clients is a renowned spinal surgeon in Brazil. He never operates until he has first filled himself with seiki. Though he wouldn't tell his medical board this, he reported to us that that his hands automatically perform their job with precision and speed once he is filled with seiki. "Seiki," he says, "is now performing the surgery." Of course, we are not saying that anyone can unconsciously do surgery or practice medicine without an education. We're illustrating how a medical education becomes supercharged and empowered with a new vitality whenever seiki is present.

We have had several spinal surgeons come to us for private healing sessions because their own spinal injuries could not be healed by medical science and previous operations. We placed them inside the currents of seiki so they could be moved by its healing vibrations. To their surprise they recovered and found relief from pain that had burdened them for years. We had nothing to do with it, other than allowing seiki to dance all of us together.

*Inside the seiki whirl things are moved in new directions: loosening, finding release, building new forms, transforming as seiki moves them to do so. Do nothing; get out of the way in order to get in the Way. Habits fall away easily when this energetic wind blows across your face. Exhausted thoughts dissipate, and worn out*

*suffering and pain wash away as seiki's weather brings a fresh rain to cleanse a torn heart. Seiki is blowin' in the wind, asking you to become the change that can change what needs to be changed.*

One of the first times Brad made a professional presentation of seiki to a group of doctors and other people-helpers, it resulted in quite a surprise. Not sure whether the audience members would be soft enough to experience seiki, he went all out in amplifying its presence. As he puts it, "I doubled the intensity of seiki that morning." To everyone's surprise, the first two rows of participants in the seminar all experienced what felt to them like spontaneous orgasms. One of the other presenters at the event was Dr. Ernest Rossi, the well-known psychotherapist and hypnotist who edited Milton H. Erickson's collected work. He observed the event and interviewed some of the people, trying to figure out what had happened. The energy in the room was so strong that even a handshake or a light touch on the back resulted in an orgasmic energetic rush for both men and women. That was the last time Brad purposefully tried to amplify seiki. From that moment on, we have allowed seiki to make up its own mind as to how strong it needs to be.

We have mentored many people all over the world in seiki jutsu. One of our seiki mentorship groups had a remarkable experience in using seiki to heal. One of the class members had a friend who had been in a coma for a year with no sign of recovering. The week we were there, the doctors at the hospital told the family to get ready for his death because he had no longer than a week to live. Our student asked one of the doctors if she and her friends could come and give their friend some prayers and healing touch. The hospital doctor said it didn't matter what they did at this point because he was beyond treatment. Several members of the class went and placed their hands on the man. They sang and shook, passing on a vibration that was inspired by caring love. To everyone's surprise, the man woke up and spoke to them. He fully recovered and went home. The doctors are still baffled over what occurred.

*What happened to him is what takes place every week in the Kalahari. He received a healing vibration. The healer didn't heal. Instead, seiki moved someone who, in turn, touched someone else so it could be shared and passed along. Healers are "vibration catchers." They catch a vibration that enables them to be tuned and then pass it on to others. We like to say that seiki work is a kind of spiritual tag. Someone catches a spiritual vibration and touches another, and that person touches someone else, continuing until everyone is touched by the spirited presence of seiki. In the game of tag you say, "You're it!" whenever you touch someone. The same is true for seiki. When it touches you, "You are it!" You become tuned and ready to share seiki.*

On a flight to South Africa Brad sat (serendipitously) next to the medical doctor who worked on the film *The Gods Must Be Crazy,* a comedy about the Bushmen. After finding out that Brad was on his way to visit the Kalahari Bushmen and that he had spent time in the village of the movie's main Bushman actor, the doctor told a story. It turns out that N!xau, the Bushman who played the lead role in the film, got very ill during the filming and was taken to a doctor for treatment. The doctor advised the film crew to drive N!xau to a hospital that was hundreds of miles away. The next thing that happened was that N!xau started trembling and shaking. The doctor thought his condition was getting worse so they ordered a plane to get him to an emergency room. When N!xau arrived at the hospital, he stopped trembling; he had spontaneously recovered. The doctor said that he still has no idea what happened to that Bushman film star. He could not see that N!xau had administered himself the world's oldest medicine—a healing vibration.

Over the years, many healers from all over the world have called on us to help them with a symptom, problem, or difficulty in their lives.

Once a medicine woman from Canada came because she had hives and sore legs that her doctor was not able to cure. Brad held her hand and filled himself with seiki. As they sat there trembling, she started telling him about a dream she recently had about a man who had died a couple of years previously. Brad quickly interrupted her and asked whether that man made jewelry. Brad reported that he was imagining a silver necklace with a particular black stone; sure enough, there was such a necklace, and it was made by the man she had dreamed. He was a jewelry maker, and he made that necklace for his wife. However, the woman who came to see us had secretly always wanted that necklace. With seiki giving us the assurance to say what we felt, we recommended that she ask the widow for the jewelry.

She later reported that when she felt the shaking vibrations, it overwhelmed her when it started. "You can feel it right away. It touches you deeply." She also later reported that "after he doctored me, my sore legs and hives cleared up . . . I felt refreshed and healthy, mentally as well as physically. I haven't forgotten it. In fact I think about it a lot. . . . There is a powerful thing happening with this medicine. I've been around a lot of healers and medicine people. I have never seen anything like it before." And she did receive the silver necklace with the black stone. It was given to her as a gift from the wife of the man she had dreamed about.

In this case, seiki brought a vision that gave instruction for what to do. This happened often with Osumi Sensei, as it does with other ecstatic healers who have a strong relationship with seiki. The woman's husband was so taken by what had happened that he also asked for a session. He was a traditional medicine man who had helped establish addiction treatment centers across Canada. He was loved by others for his kindness, generosity, and nonjudgmental character. He taught traditional spiritual wisdom to young and old alike and served as cultural director at one of the treatment centers. He liked to say that "mankind is my business." When this man came to Brad he confessed, "Though I am in the medicine way, I have a problem I have never shared with anyone. I can't even share it with you. I just want the spirits to help me with it."

Honoring his request, they went to a dark room, just as is done in a traditional ceremony of his culture. There seiki entered as Brad sang a song. The man later described his experience in an audio recording:

I had an amazing experience. I saw little lights flying around all over the place. I've seen them before in sweat lodges. I could hear Brad talking in some other language . . . I felt a tiny lightning bolt go into my head. Brad is uncanny in the way he is in tune with the spirits. Before seeing Brad, I had never had a vision. Although hard to believe for a medicine man, this was the truth and a fact of my life that I deeply wanted to change. In the ceremony Brad instructed me to place twelve twigs under my bed in the shape of a clock, to be located directly underneath my chest. The twigs were to be gathered from the woods where I live, each one collected from a different geographical direction, from north to south, east and west, and coordinates in between. Brad sent strong vibrations into me through sound and then said to me, "The spirits want to get in touch with you. You shouldn't be trying to contact *them* so much."

I had been doing this, but I had never told anyone this. It was too embarrassing to be in the medicine way and to admit that I had never had a vision. This is what I could not bring myself to tell Brad, but he knew. I followed his instruction and I have been visioning almost every night and remembering most of it. At first I was freaked out. I thought I was flying over my house. It actually scared me a bit. Since then, I've had phenomenal and fantastic visions. I have been given clear visions of my life as a child. I can now remember everything about my life, as I have flown over it through time. I have seen all of it, including the pain. My life has become amazing, for now I am a visionary dreamer. It's been that way since that ceremony.

We received a call from a woman who was a medical researcher at the Mayo Clinic in Rochester, Minnesota. She said her daughter needed help and she didn't know where else to go. Her daughter was a competitive college gymnast who had undergone knee surgery several years before. Although the best doctors at the Mayo Clinic had worked with her, they were startled to find that after she recovered from surgery she was unable to perform a forward somersault.

She was sent to various departments throughout the clinic, from surgery to physical rehabilitation to psychiatry. No matter what they tried, nothing worked. For several years, she found herself unable to move every time she attempted a forward somersault. The Mayo Clinic gave up and suggested that perhaps she should try some alternative approach. The girl's parents went on a search to find an alternative treatment for their daughter and were given the name of the Milton Erickson Foundation in Phoenix, Arizona, a world-renowned center for hypnosis and innovative work in psychotherapy. After the director of the foundation listened to their story, he recommended that they have a meeting with us.

When the young gymnast, now a college student in Wisconsin, came to our house, we told her about seiki. We directed seiki toward her knee and suggested that she start moving her body in a way that would attract seiki to flow through her whole being. After one week, she returned and said she felt a tingling in her knee throughout the week, and that to her great surprise, and her coach's surprise, she had spontaneously done a double somersault during a practice session. One week of seiki was able to bring what years of medical treatment were unable to accomplish.

As we continued teaching her more about dancing with seiki, we had a session where she spontaneously visualized a special box her grandmother had once given her. Since we were full of seiki, we trusted what came up in our intuition and advised that she should be on the lookout for a dream in which she might encounter this box. The very next night she dreamed of the box and heard a voice tell her to open it. She did, and found that it held a tiny snake, all coiled up. This didn't frighten her, but it made her curious. We told her that cultures throughout the world depict the snake as a symbol of the vital life force.

We asked her to keep track of her dreams for the following week and to choose one word for each dream that would best represent the meaning it had. For the dream she just had, she chose the word *snake.* When she returned to the next session, she was delighted to report that she had experienced three powerful dreams.

The first dream involved a frightening criminal entering her house. In the dream, she hid in the closet and covered herself with a pile of clothes. When the intruder opened the closet door and lifted off the clothes, he looked at her and said, "There is no one here." He then left, and she was not harmed in any way. The word for that dream was *fear,* and we discussed how the last several years of her life had been filled with the fear that she would never be able to perform a gymnastic routine again. For three years she had sought help in numerous forms, but she had not competed in a single competition. In this dream, however, she faced fear, and it did not come in.

The second night she dreamed of being near the edge of a canyon. There she turned into a cloud and was able to fly over the canyon, and over a forest that was right next to it. Her word for that dream was *cloud,* and it captured her feeling of being weightless and able to fly without effort.

In the third dream she had that week, she saw herself in a gymnastic competition performing her routine with absolute perfection. She chose the words *desired reality* to capture the essence of that dream and noted that she experienced complete ecstasy in the dream.

At our request, our client then took the words she had chosen for her dreams and constructed a sentence with them that would capture what she had learned from seiki. The sentence she came up with was this: "When you see the coiled *snake,* know that some will see *fear,* while you will see the secret to life, the seiki that turns you into a weightless *cloud* and effortlessly moves you to your *desired reality.*" She decided to focus on this sentence whenever she was about to perform her gymnastic routine. The next evening she performed for the first time in three years. She placed in two of her events and led her team to first place.

One of the leading philosophers of bodywork, Don Hanlon Johnson, underscores how the invention of different body therapies arises from the originator's own spontaneous movements, which too easily become rigidified when they become formalized and taught to others in a fixed manner. The most promising future for body therapy will be in the direction of returning us to an experience of basic, natural movements that take place effortlessly and spontaneously.

One of the early pioneers of using spontaneous body movement as a therapeutic practice was Dr. David Akstein, a psychiatrist from Rio de Janeiro. He studied how some of the ecstatic spiritual traditions of Brazil, especially *umanda* and *candomblé*, used spontaneous movement to induce an altered experience, what he called a "kinetic trance." He decided to experiment with this form of naturally induced hypnosis. He first taught some dancers with the national ballet company, Ballet Nacional do Brasil, how to move spontaneously, assuming it might help their performance. He avoided all spiritual beliefs and superstitions and only focused on helping them enter into the automatic motions. To his surprise, they not only felt invigorated and lifted in their performance, they also reported spontaneous healings. One woman who had been diagnosed with depression was suddenly symptom free; others reported a wide range of improvements, both physical and mental. This led him to introduce a new kind of movement therapy called Terpsichoretrance therapy, named after Terpsichore, the Greek goddess of dance and music. Terpsichoretrance therapy simply means "dancing trance therapy." It draws upon Dr. Akstein's background as a neuropsychiatrist and scholar of trance. Milton Erickson called Dr. Akstein one of the major figures in the history of hypnosis. Whereas Charcot, Mesmer, and others had created direct hypnosis (encouraging the subject to enter directly into a trance), and Erickson had developed indirect hypnotic suggestion, Dr. Akstein had recognized "kinetic hypnosis," trance induced by spontaneous movement.

Working with groups of psychiatric patients, Akstein played ritualistic music he had recorded and invited everyone to move spontaneously, dancing in a freely spirited fashion. He found that this kind of ecstatic dancing was a nonverbal group therapy that led to all kinds of improvements in the lives of his patients. Although the therapy is not suitable for people with epilepsy, serious cardiovascular problems, certain motion disorders, and women in the first trimester of pregnancy, it was successfully used as a therapeutic approach for people suffering from a wide range of problems, including most of the so-called psychoneurotic neuroses. The therapy also proved highly successful as a tool for personal growth and development.

In an effort to explain the therapeutic benefits of this highly aroused movement therapy, Akstein and Portal proposed that ecstatic movement helps bring forth an emotional release. As quoted in Doug Morgan's *T.T.T.: An Introduction to Trance Dancing,* "We have seen the sub-cortical areas are released from inhibition, in particular the limbic system, seat of the emotions. The emotional liberation is maintained by the very stimulating music, facilitating releases, and at the same time preventing them from being totally chaotic forms of expression, by the rhythms, which provides a certain framework."[1]

Observable emotional release is often one aspect of the healing response. What is likely happening at a more systemic level is the realignment, recalibration, or tuning of the individual's neurobehavioral organization. The balance, stability, or homeostasis of the whole brain and whole body may be articulated using many different metaphors and theories. However it is specified, spontaneous movement serves to reset the organization of our whole being. This resetting or tuning applies to all possible levels of biological processes, from neurobiology to behavior and social patterns of interaction.

Brad first met Dr. David Akstein in May 1997 at the Evolution of Hypnosis Conference in Brazil. Each of them had been invited to give a keynote address. After Brad presented his work, Dr. Akstein took the stage and publicly announced that Brad was his "spiritual son." They went off to talk, and Dr. Akstein told Brad his life story—how thrilling it was to learn from indigenous practices that utilized movement and how challenging it had been to be ostracized by his own profession. He had to leave Rio and move to France, where he continued his professional career in the land where hypnosis first prospered.

Seiki jutsu goes past being attached to either the metaphors of dance or trance but sees both as possible inside a performance of spontaneous movement. Seiki doesn't care whether you enter trance or dance, but if it happens spontaneously, then it is what it is. Seiki jutsu emphasizes the freedom to be moved by seiki, in whatever form or absence of form naturally takes place.

Spontaneous healing can even take place in dream. After working with seiki in a weeklong intensive, Brad strained his back when he moved his keyboard and sound equipment following the event. That evening, filled with seiki, he had an unusual lucid dream. He thought he was awake and was getting out of bed. In his dream he believed he was putting on his clothes, and as he sat on the edge of the bed to put on his shoes, he was shocked to see a scorpion inside one of his shoes. He had a pronounced startle response and jerked back. At that moment, in the instant motion, he spontaneously gave his spine an adjustment. He woke up and found his back pain gone.

Years later when Brad's knee gave him some trouble, he went into seiki and asked what he should do about it. He heard an inner voice tell him to include more calamari in his diet. The knee pain disappeared. Seiki is the doctor, the voice, and the movement needed to guide us into realignment, tuning, and healing.

Dr. Andrew Weil once wrote that "if medicine is to come back in alignment with the great healing traditions and satisfy the needs and desires of those who are sick, it must recover the truths that Bob Fulford expresses."[2] Brad was a friend of Dr. Fulford. They discussed how the vital life force was the main truth of his practice and of the practice of all great healers throughout the world. Dr. Fulford wanted to see medicine follow the trail of healing vibrations. When Brad showed him seiki jutsu, he was thrilled to exclaim that seiki, the vital life force, rather than synthetic or natural drugs, holds the most promising future of medicine. He said that seiki jutsu "marks the beginning of an awakening of the universal life force that is accessible to everyone . . . It is time for each of us to be acquainted with this energizing force and bring it into our daily life."

Brad also showed Dr. Fulford a particular hands-on way of giving a special vibration. It involves the left hand being placed just above the person's heart while the right hand is on the back shoulder behind the heart. Vibrations are then allowed to pulse in a spontaneous way and automatically start when performed by a master of seiki jutsu. The vibrations in the left and right hands are usually different, often polyrhythmic and syncopated. They are usually gentle but pronounced and awaken a high frequency. If you are soft and prepared, the vibrations will typically spread throughout your body, and the effects are immediate and often dramatic.

After that demonstration, Dr. Fulford concluded that it was the key to healing that he had spent his whole career trying to find. In a letter, he wrote, "I have found your technique of starting first [with] working the left shoulder and heart area to be very effective in treating. It seems to unlock the rest of the problems." He said further that this way of transmitting a vibration was the highest form of healing he had ever experienced. It brought forth the highest frequencies of spiritual vibration that spread through the lower, embedded frequencies associated with mental and physical phenomena. In the last years of his life, Dr. Fulford treated everyone with this method.

Stephen and Robin Larsen, autobiographers of Joseph Campbell, once hosted a healing service conducted by Brad at their retreat center near Woodstock, New York. A terminally ill man was carried in on a stretcher. He was in his final days of life, and he wanted to experience joy one more time before he passed away. He was unable to lift a finger and was as white as a ghost. It appeared that he might die at any moment. With a group of friends and community around him, seiki was awakened so that the room became highly charged. When Brad doctored him with infusions of seiki, he experienced a tremendous shift in his energy. He raised himself up and started singing songs from the musical *Jesus Christ Superstar,* in which he had played the role of Jesus earlier in his life. He found his voice filled with a vitality he hadn't experienced in a long time. He shouted with joy, claiming to never have felt so alive as this. He even proclaimed, "I want to make love with a Japanese woman!" No one knew exactly why he said that, but it was celebrated, for he was feeling alive, and the same seiki circulating in him was felt by everyone. He lived a couple of months longer and then left this world, happy and content.

Brad's father once was struck by a debilitating disease that no doctor could diagnose. Brad filled himself with seiki, performed its tuning movements, and fell into a dream that night. He saw himself placing his hands over his father's neck and feeling a pain that needed liberation. After Brad woke up, he made arrangements to travel to his father's town and held a ceremony for him. His grandmother first prayed and sang a hymn, and then Brad placed his hands on his father's neck, feeling a great heat enter it. His dad could feel it as well and announced that he was better. Brad took his father to a leading neurologist; after more diagnostic scans were examined, the doctor recognized what was going on and said that it was a miracle that Brad's father was still alive. A growth was starting to sever his spinal cord. They performed surgery that week, and his father lived another 20 years.

We saw a man in Puebla, Mexico, who volunteered for us to work with him in front of a group of professional practitioners. He started by saying that he had over one hundred symptoms. He even had a list of all the symptoms that doctors and therapists had diagnosed, ranging from growths in his mouth to a plentitude of behavioral and emotional issues. Hillary reached for his hand and took him into the seiki current. As we were all moving together, she asked who else in the family had carried all this suffering before him. To everyone's surprise, his late aunt had had the same condition, and that woman's aunt (one of her mother's sisters) had had it before her, and he believed the condition extended at least one more generation farther back in his lineage. His family was very worried about him. We asked him if he could say one thing to his family, what it would be. He replied, "I want them to know that I am all right. Whereas my aunts felt hopeless about their condition, I do not let sickness bring my spirit down." He was more concerned about those people around him who worried too much about his health. He prayed that they would not suffer due to his problems.

Seiki then filled our voices, and we began to chant and sing that he was like a saint, more worried about others than he was himself. As we were all moving in a circular motion, without thinking Hillary said, "For the rest of your life, you are never to call these symptoms or problems. They are to be called your *aunts*. You have become part of a lineage that carries a burden, but you do so in a way that is different from the others. You have allowed your burden to make your heart bigger, carrying hope and concern for others. This, in some unexplainable way, will help free your aunts, wherever they are in the heavens. You, who carry all the aunts, must tell them they are free and that this no longer has to be carried by others in a way that is sad and hopeless. Things have now changed. You have resolved what has long been unresolved."

The man began to weep and disclosed that he felt close to his aunts and always imagined that they were around him. "Yes, of course they are," we responded in song. Now he was very full of seiki and vibrating as we all held hands inside its movements. "I feel something moving in me," he said. "I no longer feel confused about my sickness. I have come to free my aunts and my family, free them from unnecessary concern and hopelessness."

"This is wonderful," we added. "Why don't you start celebrating your aunts now that you no longer will speak of symptoms!"

"Yes, that feels right. I can feel them rejoicing with me!"

Hillary continued, "Today is their second birthday. Each aunt, there must be at least one hundred of them over all the years, is being reborn today. Remember this date. Celebrate their birthday on this date every year."

"I will and I will sing for them tonight," he said, as he began to hum a folk song.

"Be an example to others who come to you with their pain. Tell them not to call them problems, symptoms, or disease. Tell them about the aunts. They may also need to know about the uncles, parents, grandparents, siblings, and all the relatives and friends that they carry within them. Free them so they, too, can celebrate and sing."

The whole audience was weeping by this time, and someone started singing with a deeply heartfelt tone. Others joined in. Soon the whole audience had transformed itself into a seiki community that celebrated newfound life. After the session, everyone in the group went home with a new holiday added to their schedule. In November, we celebrate Aunt's Day, the time when suffering becomes alchemically transformed into relational gold, freeing us to sing even when we feel pain and suffering.

*With seiki you are moved to move with people, asking them to dance with seiki. Here there is no bodywork, medicine, or healing. There is only movement. Everything can change—including you and the name of whatever you think is organizing your life. Symptoms can become aunts and dying can deliver the truest living. There is no need to fix anything. Instead, move and change with it. The problem with problems and the suffering in suffering is that we relate to it in one way: seek out and destroy! Seiki comes to remind you that you have an infinitude of possibilities when it comes to relating to whatever experiences come your way.*

*Viktor Frankl found this out while imprisoned in Auschwitz. There he discovered that meaning can be constructed in all circumstances and situations, even the most oppressive and horrific.*

*Like Mother Teresa, utilize whatever is given to you, transforming it into a gift that can contribute to your creating a meaningful life.*

Once Brad was interrupted at a weekend intensive by a woman who shouted out from the audience, "I have cancer and need to have a session with you now." When she came on stage, Brad was already full of seiki, remembering that he had dreamt the night before that he would see this woman and ask her this question, "Have you recently moved your furniture?" When he asked her this, she said she had just rearranged her house because her father had passed away and she had obtained some of the family furniture and heirlooms. Brad went on to ask, as he rocked back and forth in his chair, "If you had to place your cancer somewhere in the house, where would it be located?" She mentioned a particular spot in the basement. He asked her to imagine what it would look like sitting there and asked whether it would be covered up. She replied that she imagined it wrapped in old newspaper.

Brad then inquired whether it was wrapped in the classified ads, for, after all, he said with a smile, "this is 'classified information.'" As the movements raised the intensity of his voice, Brad became inspired to ask her to make a big change in her relationship with cancer. He asked her to consider placing an ad in the newspaper offering her cancer for sale. The woman felt a surge of seiki shoot through her and began rocking gently. Now they were both inside the enhanced life force currents, dancing with it together.

She shared how she had dreamed of a friend she hadn't seen for many years. In the dream, her friend gave her a Bento box. Brad teased her, saying, "That's because you are out to lunch." They then discussed seiki jutsu and the Japanese healer from Japan, Osumi Sensei. As seiki grew in the session, it inspired considering more ways of how she could move things around in her house and creatively relate to her cancer. She was then directed to begin moving herself in the seiki way, doing it at home regularly, so things could be freer to move and change.

After the session, without telling anyone, the woman actually did place an ad in the Toronto newspaper, advertising her cancer and offering it for sale. To her surprise her condition improved, and her doctor told her she would live a long life. Even more unexpected was the report that she had gone to her basement and found an ugly abstract painting wrapped in newspapers, sitting in the same spot where she had indicated that her cancer was metaphorically located. She also met the woman she had seen in her dream, whom she hadn't seen since they were adolescents. Out of the blue, her old friend called and invited her to lunch. The friend asked if she had seen or heard about the newspaper ad others were talking about—someone had placed an ad trying to sell her cancer. The news coming back to her about the action she had secretly taken in advertising her cancer for sale sent another lightning bolt of energy through her. She made a pledge to live for all the surprises and gifts that life could bring, and to keep moving with all of it.

The therapeutics of seiki spontaneous movement is that it helps free you to relate to everything, including your pain and illness, with movement. In movement are found the seeds of change, the roots of alchemy, and the original source of whole healing. Come to seiki with no expectation other than changing anything and everything, doing so because seiki asks you to dance with whatever is moving in front of your very eyes. Grab hold of seiki's hands, whoever is embodying it, and take a step or two as part of life's unpredictable choreography. Do it to feel totally alive.

# 6

# SEIKI CONVERSATION
## The New Future of the Talking Cure

The vital life force becomes enhanced and fully non-subtle when it pervades your whole being. To fill your heart with seiki, your voice must also pulse in a new way, becoming another pump that brings the life force both up and down the body.

With seiki, your voice becomes empowered in an exhilarating way. Seiki is pumped by a contraction in your belly, sending it up your spine; at the same time, seiki is flowing from the crown of your head downward. But while it may seem that there are two lines of seiki flowing up and down, side by side, really there is one main line and it goes in all directions. Feel it everywhere, including your legs, arms, fingertips, neck, and vocal cords. Without an ecstatic voice that carries a seiki vibration, things cannot reach the desired crescendo, even though action is strong and involves an impressive display. The heart must be inspired by a voice that pierces it with sound, rhythm, poetics, and song. Conversation becomes electrified with seiki, ready to change people's lives. Prepare to awaken and open your voice to express seiki.

Seiki is an essential yet absent ingredient in contemporary forms of the so-called talking cure—whether administered as therapy, coaching, counseling, consulting, or some other form. All these professionalized talk-based practices are in desperate need of being led by seiki rather than theory and ideology. When you watch therapists being portrayed on television and film, they typically offer clichéd, predictable lines that a computer-programmed robot could just as well offer. If the observant critic who noticed that the emperor wears no clothes was to comment, we might hear that most therapeutic talk is boring and dead.

*It's time to stop the broken record from repeating: "How do you feel about that?" "Can you say more about that?" "What do you think that's about?" Let's take a break from talking about solutions, problems, narratives, psychodynamics, behavioral strategies, cognitive patterns, personality types, and everything else that has built the mile-high tower of psychobabble. It is likely more resourceful to burn a professional license and talk like a human being again. Even better, cover that mental health license with honey and hang it from a string. As it's kept busy catching flies, its owner can take a break and catch a wave of seiki-inspired flight. Ask the creative life force to participate more in transformative conversation. It may want to redecorate a conversational space with curios that encourage unexpected exploration. Have a fishing pole in the corner with a wisdom quotation hanging from its line, a teddy bear sitting upright in a chair holding a flashlight, or a tiny kite hanging from the ceiling with a tail made of fortune cookies. Try talking about a butterfly that didn't want to leave the net, an acorn that dropped from a tree, or the man who lived in a can because he couldn't see past his plan. Prescribe eating a bowl of Rice Krispies so that some snap, crackle, and pop can be heard again. Or recommend a family vacation for the pet dog—don't forget to take pictures so there's a scrapbook of that special day or*

*weekend. Remind someone that he can be the first person in the world to carry an antenna in his briefcase for receiving and/or transmitting hope—perhaps it's a string wrapped around a map of Cape Hope or a soft wire that is covered with hay, for haywire can inspire a desire to conspire a spitfire that can conquer any quagmire, vampire, or hellfire.*

Only seiki can bring talk back to life—more broadly, seiki brings *life* into all conversations, especially those that involve a person seeking help and guidance. Whether you are a therapist or bartender, friend or relative, neighbor or carpool passenger, when someone comes to you for help you need seiki to give them life-to-life resuscitation. With seiki you hunt for and feed that which brings a connection to vital living, creative innovation, divine mystery, or whatever name you wish to call that which inspires transformative change.

Because seiki is not limited to residing inside any school of professional rhetoric, it does not discriminate between what is therapeutic conversation and what isn't, nor does it give any importance to the differentiation between bodywork and talk therapy. Seiki crosses all borders without restriction. It can flow into any human encounter—spoken or unspoken, active or still, professional or public, and transform all participants by its presence. Seiki-inspired talk may take place anywhere and be expressed by anyone, but when articulated in a setting whose purpose is helping others with their existential suffering, it becomes a healing balm.

Over the years we have helped many therapists and professional people-helpers from all over the world get a healing heart by awakening them with seiki. We encourage them to move from therapy to healing, allowing seiki to speak through them rather than offer the patter of imitative discourse. With seiki it becomes clear that therapeutic talk is never separate from bodywork. When you talk to people, you do so with the vibrations of your vocal cords, and their bodies listen and respond in kind. Talking itself is bodywork—there is no such thing as talk without a moving body. While we can distinguish between mind and body as metaphors to indicate how we sometimes experience them as separate, all of life involves the body's voice and the voiced body.

It is unfortunate that the professions of bodywork and talk therapy are separated by professional organizations, for it is an arbitrary division that may perpetuate mind-body dualisms rather than heal them. At the same time, when healing is set free from theoretical restrictions, we still find that there are sessions that sometimes involve more body movement and less talk, just as there are times when talk overrides expressive movement. We have worked and taught in a wide range of venues, from holistic clinics to psychotherapy clinics, schools, prisons, churches, temples, shamanic circles, live theatre, and cabaret. Each setting provides contextual cues that communicate the nature of what typically takes place inside that setting, and this does influence the performance. It is time for seiki, rather than regulatory professional organizations, to decide what is best for healing, and to mend the dismemberment of the body that professional distinctions erroneously enforce.

*Try this little experiment: take the letter "b" from the word "body" and exchange it with the letter "m" from the word "mind." Now you have two new words, "mody" and "bind." For one week use these words every day so you are able to experience yourself talking about how your "bind" thinks and your "mody" moves. Consider this one step toward bending and mending the "bind-mody" split. Be "bindful" in this meditation and give your "mody" a good workout.*

The beginning challenge of therapeutic or change-oriented conversation—whether carried out in psychotherapy, family therapy, counseling, social work, or coaching settings—is to not forget that there are bodies in the room, and that the voice, as part of the body, has a wide range of movement and expression. The interaction of free movement and spontaneous, seiki-inspired talk is the future of the talking cure—not as a collection of forms or techniques, but as a performance that arises naturally out of an authentic relationship with seiki. The latter brings us back to the old wisdom ways of healing and takes us past the limitations and unnecessary restrictions of habituated routines.

We often work with clients when they are sitting in front of us on a seiki bench. We typically reach over to hold their hands whenever seiki starts waking us up. We may place a tremor in the palm of the client's hand as we talk, wiggle a finger, or lift her arm and move it around in spontaneous motion. As we sit, we are rocking, bobbing, and sometimes shaking. We will be talking to the client the whole time, letting our voices and words carry and transmit the seiki energy as much as our bodies.

*Ask that your voice be set free. It desires more than humdrum talk and being a drone. Give it the throne it deserves and let more vibrant sound be found in your everyday. If you want to be of sound mind, then ask your body to voice it. If you want to embody life, then never mind what you said before. Open your mouth as you open your heart. Both must be open to find your Beethoven. Your unfinished movement requires an awakened voice that brings you more choice in how you rejoice.*

It is seiki that brings forth the particular expression of a transformative performance. If seiki isn't pulsing within you, you can't authentically deliver its energized expression. Shouting ecstatically or trembling your body will not foster a seiki-filled session if it is purposefully simulated rather than spontaneously created. You have to get out of the way and let seiki do the walking and talking. As Zora Neale Hurston so aptly said, "Those that don't got it, can't show it. Those that got it, can't hide it." If it looks and feels as if seiki is absent, then it is. When you are filled with seiki, it will shine through no matter what you say or do.

The oldest teaching for healers is simply to fill yourself with the vital life force and then get out of the way. Seiki will kick out boring psychobabble, clichéd lines, and the lifeless routines of any model. It will pave the way for improvisation of the whole of you in relationship to the whole of your clients. It is not possible to be an instrument that serves others in a sacred way without letting go of the inner clutter and becoming empty and available for seiki to have its voice.

Recall how we discussed that the three steps of the seiki exercise become only one step when seiki is mastered. Catching a rhythm, improvising, and entering the seiki tuning zone are ultimately inseparable. The same applies to the distinction between bodywork and therapeutic conversation. When you are a master of either, both become integrated so that you never know whether sound or silence, movement or stillness will be performed in a session. It's always improvised, outside your conscious will and in the hands of a greater power—the natural flow of seiki. It all comes down to this teaching: When seiki lives inside of you, life will happen spontaneously and deliver all kinds of wonderful mysteries.

Seiki-inspired therapeutic conversation never concerns itself with diagnosis, so no one is given psychological assessments to determine whether they are depressed, anxious, psychotic, or whatever. The idea that you must first assess in order to know what to do is out of tune to a seiki practitioner; instead, you become full of seiki and allow things to be improvised. You may be inspired to invent a diagnosis that helps get things moving, like we did with an artistically inclined client who was stuck in his life and hadn't painted in a long time. We told him that he had a constipated hand that needed a paintbrush to release the creative expression that was wanting to come out.

With seiki you become an improvisationalist, an experimental performer in a Life Force Theatre of infinite possibilities. Here you step on stage and immediately make some motion that aims to change clients, and then utilize whatever response they have in order to adjust how you try encouraging them to shift all over again. This emphasis on change is open to any resourceful means of freeing people from whatever impedes their moving forward with life.

When we speak of change we are referring to both the practitioner and the client. In seiki, it takes a changing practitioner to bring forth a changing client. We used to supervise therapy in a graduate program while sitting behind a one-way mirror watching a session conducted by a student therapist. Our role was to cue the client to suggest things that could be said to wake up the therapist. For example, we might suggest a client inquire of the therapist: "What might you ask about my closet that you have never considered asking?" We aim to help the client inspire the therapist to change as the therapist assists the client to make her own transformations.

When the practitioner is full of the vital life force, his senses are more highly responsive to the communications of the client. Arguably the most important communications are unconscious and bring forth automatic responses of the practitioner. Similarly, when the client is brought more deeply inside of seiki, she will also speak and act more spontaneously. As both client and practitioner interact spontaneously, both of their habituated minds take a time out, enabling the rest of their whole beings to more fully participate.

Keep in mind that the seiki practitioner gives no importance to stopping the ongoing flow of thoughts and images. If an idea arises spontaneously it is expressed, but given no invitation to remain as a static fixture in the conversation should another idea follow it. This way of improvising ideation, talk, and body movement enable all realms of experience to be spontaneous. Improvised performance rather than informed redundancy drives the encounter. At the same time, the seiki practitioner's spontaneous presence is organized by feeding a virtuous circle in the client's life situation and in the session: all talk and movement aims to soften a client, wiggle them out of stuck habits and thoughts, and help them step inside a bigger horizon. Thus a skilled practitioner works improvisationally to maintain interactional presence inside the vital life force, so that seiki may orchestrate how a session moves.

Seiki-inspired conversation is jazz. It cannot help but contribute to promoting change for it is always changing. In its improvisation there is only an ever-changing song. As Nick Tosches reminds us in his book *Where Dead Voices Gather*:

> And, of course, that is what all of this is—all of this: the one song, ever changing, ever reincarnated, that speaks somehow from and to and for that which is ineffable within us and without us, that is both prayer and deliverance, folly and wisdom, that inspires us to dance or smile or simply to go on, senselessly, incomprehensibly, beatifically, in the face of mortality and the truth that our lives are more ill-writ, ill-rhymed and fleeting than any song, except perhaps those songs—that song, endlessly reincarnated—born of that truth, be it the moon and June of that truth, or the wordless blue moan, or the rotgut or the elegant poetry of it. That nameless black-hulled ship of Ulysses, that long black train, that Terraplane, that mystery train, that Rocket "88," that Buick 6—same journey, same miracle, same end and endlessness.[1]

Seiki jutsu, always on the move, does not propagate static beliefs that therapists and coaches sometimes cling to in their practice. For example, many somatic and movement-oriented therapists believe that traumatic experience from the past is stored in the somatic system, and that either choreographed or improvised movement can offer a release from an historically stuck emotional burden. In seiki jutsu this idea, and any other idea, is not necessary as an operating premise. Whether or not it is true is considered less relevant than allowing seiki to direct a spontaneous interaction with the client. Should a client have a flashback to an early experience—whether it is assumed to be repressed memories of pain or bliss—it is not regarded as having any particular dominant meaning. Instead, the experience is simply nothing more or less than a part of the ongoing performance. Though it is likely that such experiences arise in part from the belief system of a client who may think she is repressing past traumas and needs them released, the practitioner of seiki jutsu is not distracted by proving or attending to any singular frame of meaning. Like an advanced Bushman n/om-kxao, a seiki jutsu master is ready to hold and release any attribution of meaning, utilizing the semantic domain only when it arises spontaneously in real time interaction.

*Before helping someone, it is wise to initiate a seiki exercise, getting yourself into the rhythmic pulse, improvisational flow, and the seiki tuning zone that fosters spontaneous healing interaction. If you are buzzing with seiki, all else will follow. Of course this may seem easier said than done. Realize that when you are fully charged with seiki, you are in the highest state of being alive and this includes being a resourceful, creative, ethical, and transformative agent of change. Everything comes together in enhanced seiki, including all the important considerations of your being someone who can help others.*

We teach our clinical graduate students how to bring spirited expression and improvisation into their work, sometimes saying that if a session doesn't have any life force or spirit, then it is dead. In other words, their talk and presence needs an infusion of seiki. Once we were interrupted in class by the clinical director knocking on the classroom door with an emergency request—someone was in the parking lot needing to be seen by a therapist. The person had held a gun to his head the night before with the intention of committing suicide, but at the last moment he opened his Bible to read some scripture. He then decided to live another day and to try seeing a therapist. We immediately brought him into the clinic and listened to him tell one of the most riveting and tragic stories we had ever heard. He had had a successful career at a sporting goods store, where he oversaw the sales of fishing and hunting gear, but due to his knees giving out he could no longer work. In a matter of months he had lost everything, including his wife, family, job, and health. He had hit bottom and didn't know what to do next.

While his story was catastrophic, his voice had tremendous life in it. He told his story with great passion and gusto. When he was finished, our first response to him was, "We feel like we are sitting in a large auditorium listening to you give an amazing inspirational speech. We know that if you were speaking in front of a big church congregation right now, everyone would be on the edge of their seats, waiting to hear what happened next in the life of this extraordinary man. You have told the first part of your story that depicts how your life fell apart. Now we are wondering what you will say about how you brought yourself back from the edge of defeat and into the future, turning your life around."

Before he could answer, we continued. "Given the circumstance you are in, can we be totally straight with you?" After he nodded yes, we asked, "Do you think there is anyone out there in the world who is worse off than you?"

"Oh yes, there certainly are, and I know some of them. Like those men that live underneath the bridge."

We felt ourselves full of seiki at this point, and Brad's voice took on the sound of a preacher. "Are you aware that the Bible says that Jesus calls us to be fishers of men?"

The man nearly jumped out of his seat and trembled, as he said with tears in his eyes, "Last night when I was ready to end my life, I just opened my Bible at random to see what it would say. That is the exact verse that I saw when I opened the book: Mark, chapter 1, verse 17: '. . . and I will make you fishers of men.' Why, it's a miracle that you mentioned that verse. It's what saved my life."

"Since you're a man with expertise in both hunting and fishing, we can see what has happened. You picked up the wrong tool. Jesus didn't say 'pick up a gun.' He asked you to pick up a fishing pole. Your mission is clear."

"Yes it is." He nodded enthusiastically.

"You must become a fisher of men. Get out some fishing poles and go help those men under the bridge, or whoever else you choose to help, catch themselves a meal. An edible meal and a holy meal."

"Yes! You are right. I have plenty of fishing poles, and I know a homeless man I've been meaning to help for many years," he said with an increased enthusiasm.

We continued talking about how he could help others who were less fortunate than he, and how he should be reaching for a fishing pole in order to do it. At the end, he was so moved by the session that he said, "The holy spirit has been with us. I know he sent me here. Can we get on our knees and pray?"

We got on our knees and held hands, while Brad prayed in a way that would speak to the man's beliefs and heart: "Dear Lord, we are deeply and humbly moved by what we have witnessed here today. The power of your reach, the depth of your wisdom, and the grace of your love have made a miracle happen in this room and in this man. We ask that he never forget what the holy spirit led him to last night. You, sir, are being asked to be a fisher of men. You, sir, are being asked to reach for your fishing pole and help those who are in great need. We remember all those disciples who were close to your precious son, and how they suffered in order to be brought closer to the truths that set them free and brought them to the kingdom of God. We say thank you for everything, including our trials and tribulations, as they have brought us closer to you. Bless this man and his fishing pole, and all the knowledge and caring he can give to those who need him to offer a helping hand. Bless him for the authority his voice conveys in telling his testimony. We ask that his story now become more intertwined and embraced by your story, the greatest story ever told. In the name of our savior and precious Lord we say tonight and forevermore, Amen and Amen." The man wept but continued to glow, filled with seiki—what he recognized as the holy spirit. We, too, were touched, and our hearts felt renewed. In the presence of seiki, holiness may arrive to offer comfort and hope to those who are weary and lost, doing so in a way that helps them celebrate the mysterious paradox that teaches us that sometimes you have to lose your life in order to find it.

*Open whatever sacred book you find meaningful. Turn to a random page or passage and write down whatever sentence you see. Do this two more times. Select the one sentence that has the most energy for you when you read it. Carry this sentence with you for a week. Act as if these words are saving your life. Turn the words into a spontaneous song. Make sure you sing it three times a day, even if you have to whisper your musical rendition. Ask the words and the song to become a line for seiki to travel on.*

We have a track record of seeing "impossible" cases, clients whom other therapists have worked with and feel stuck in treating or healing. One man had been institutionalized for over forty years in a mental hospital, diagnosed as a schizophrenic with brain damage. His parents had never heard him utter a single sentence that wasn't gibberish or nonsense. At a Bible college in Arkansas, we were asked to see the man with his parents, as an audience of therapists and pastors observed in a different room. Most of the audience had actually seen this client during their training years at one mental health center or another.

As Brad walked toward the clinical room he saw an artificial tree sitting in the hall for decoration. He spontaneously picked it up and carried it into the room. Plopping it down in front of the man, Brad then dropped to his knees and without introducing himself said, "What if I only had five more minutes to live. What could you tell me now that would make a difference in my life?" To everyone's surprise, the man spoke clearly, offering wise counsel infused with teachings from the Bible. His parents were in shock; both of them had tears in their eyes. We asked them, "Did you hear that? Why isn't he teaching? Why isn't he at least teaching Sunday school? Do you see that he could?"

The parents nodded in agreement that their son was capable of doing more than playing the role of a so-called schizophrenic. We went on to tell the man that he should not throw away his other talent that enabled him to confuse and confound others. But while that could sometimes come in handy, he also needed to start expressing the other talents he possessed. We found out that this man had a natural way of being around cats and that cats liked him. Since he was full of religious knowledge, we encouraged him to become an evangelist to cats, and then later he could decide whether he wanted to move on to other critters, whether those included people or not. He agreed, but pointed out that he wasn't ordained as a preacher.

"No problem, we have many preachers around here, and they can ordain you. Hold on, we'll be back in a moment." We walked back to the auditorium where there were at least two dozen preachers in the audience. We asked for volunteers, and most of those preachers came forward. We asked them to come into the clinical room. One by one, they laid their hands on the man and offered a blessing for his ministry. No one objected, for they had already been deeply moved by what they saw and wanted to be a part of this healing moment.

The miracle of that day had not only to do with the transformations in the client but also involved what happened to the clergy when they entered the room. As they participated in this impromptu blessing and ordination service, they felt a current of electricity surge through their bodies. Many of them exclaimed that it was the first time they had truly felt the holy spirit. They had preached about it, thought they knew it, but until they experienced its high voltage in that room, they had never been physically touched by it. The miracle is that the man, deemed crazy by most professionals who had seen him, changed the lives of dozens of ministers in Arkansas. He helped bring them the holy spirit.

In another training intensive, Hillary told the group that the next client would be handed a bottle and asked, "Have you ever received a message in a bottle?" On the inside of the bottle would be a piece of paper with this question written on it that was inspired by the seiki circulating in us: "What happened to your pet bunny?" The client was a former addict who had run a meth lab before he was arrested and ordered by the court to see us. We handed him the bottle, and he read its message.

Sure enough, it turns out that he had had a very special pet bunny as a child and was so close to it that when it died, he gave it a funeral. That wasn't the only pet he had. As a child and young adult his house had been full of all kinds of animals, including uncaged birds. He had even rescued a raccoon that became his pet and was practiced at resting on his shoulder. The young man developed quite a reputation among his friends and family for his affinity with animals.

As the details surrounding the uniqueness of this man's life unfolded, seiki was palpable in the room. His demeanor changed, and he came to life as he told us one animal story after another. Another question popped into our mind. It was the day after the presidential election, so Hillary asked, "If animals rather than people had been allowed to vote, we bet you would have been elected president. What you do think?"

"Yes, I believe that would be the case. I have a gift with animals. I can communicate with them. They come to me. Once I sat on a park bench and a wild squirrel walked up and jumped in my lap. It stood there and looked into my eyes. I never heard of that before, and I wouldn't believe it if I heard it about someone else. But it happened to me."

When we asked whether he still had a household of pets, he said that stopped several years ago, about the time he got involved in meth. We heard that his life was resourceful and positive during the times when animals surrounded him. It should be no surprise that we prescribed a special task for him, asking him to take a walk in the woods as soon as he could, carrying the bottle that held the message. He was to announce as loudly as he could to all the animals, "I'm back." We added that he would know what to do after that because the animals would help him bring back what he once had, but had forgotten.

*Go to a special place that you regard as holy. It could be a cathedral, state park, lake, museum, or anywhere else at all. Make a special trip there and say out loud, "I'm back." Say it several times, voicing it differently each time. Announce it as if seiki is there waiting to hear you say this in a way that indicates that you sincerely desire to meet and greet seiki.*

When you are full of seiki, it is possible to quickly change the life of anyone, including someone who is serving time in prison. We saw a young male prisoner who had given up all hope. As we sat in a secure room with him, we started to rock with seiki. After a brief conversation in which we found out that he had just gone through some vocational training that taught him how to install an electrical light, we asked if he was proud of that skill. His mood started to change, and he mentioned that he was being asked to install lights all over the prison because of his natural aptitude for electrical work. We then invited him to call himself the Light Man. He liked this new name and decided to make himself a business card with this name on it, something he could easily do at the print shop. He also mentioned that he would draw a lightbulb on his "business card" and that he would use it in the future when he needed to get a job.

We changed our tone and leaned over to deliver this instruction. "We'd like for you to draw a lightbulb right now on this piece of paper." When he did that, we proceeded. "Now take this lightbulb and place it under your pillow tonight before you go to sleep." We said this in a way that marked it as a holy act that was meant especially for him.

The following week this young man had a glow on his face. He could barely wait to tell us that something amazing had happened. After placing that picture of a lightbulb under his pillow, he went to sleep and was awakened in the middle of the night. He experienced a vision where he was in a boat with an old man. They were in a swamp filled with alligators. The old man in the dream handed him a light and said, "Shine it on those gators, and I'll show you how to not be afraid." Then the man said, "I'll be back."

Sure enough, each night he slept with the lightbulb drawing under his pillow, the old man came back to him in his dreams and continued to teach, guide, and heal him. The young man's life changed, and others in the prison began calling him the Light Man. Another prisoner wrote a song for him. He started helping other young men who were struggling. The old man in his dreams taught him what to do.

*Go ahead and draw your own sketch of a lightbulb and place it under your pillow. Others have, and they got themselves a sweet holy teaching. Make sure that you do everything you can to infuse seiki into this bulb, to help light it up when you are asleep. Turn on some music that touches your soul as you prepare to draw it. Choose the right color of pen and paper. Cut it out and sprinkle it with water while giving it a blessing. Hold it while conducting a seiki performance. Doctor it so it will attract seiki into your dreaming.*

As each of our case stories illustrates, it is possible to fill yourself with seiki before you meet a client, including one you know nothing about, and be given guidance as to what to say. This is typical for most great healers and can happen to anyone who gets well seasoned by seiki.

Unexpected things happen frequently when seiki organizes your conversation. Not only does the enhanced life force foster a more spirited encounter with another, it alters the way ideas come into your mind. You receive a hookup to your clients that cannot be explained. Call it clairvoyance, intense intuition, spiritual help, or whatever else. What matters is that seiki brings these experiences and makes them natural, with no need for explanation. Whatever happens just happens, and you use it to help others. Most importantly, the authenticity and sweet fragrance of gentle kindness and love must permeate your movement, sound, and song.

We recognize that there are times when people will naively think they are filled with seiki and ready to teach and heal others. This happens quite frequently with beginners. When any amount of seiki enters you, it brings with it such a dramatic shift that you may be tempted to think that you have been completely filled by seiki. Here trickster mind and ego step in and encourage you to claim an authority and expertise that has not yet ripened.

This is why elders long familiar with the mastery of seiki need to be present in one's development. You need to be kept on the straight and narrow path, the seiki line that is recognizable to others who have walked it many times. In addition, there are signs that help to indicate whether you are ready to bring forth movements and talk that can help transform others. We discuss these in the following chapter on seiki jutsu mentorship.

# 7

# BEING MENTORED IN SEIKI JUTSU

Students have arrived from all over the world, ready to be immersed in seiki jutsu. They have traveled from Cape Town, Rio, Mexico City, New York, San Francisco, Phoenix, Los Angeles, Boulder, Toronto, Chicago, Atlanta, Santa Fe, and from small towns and remote areas. It is time for a special intensive with seiki jutsu to begin, another gathering of our experiential mentorship program. As people enter The Keeney Institute for Healing, we know they will soon feel like a tribe, a family that comes from diverse lineages that have all led to finding the deepest mysteries of the non-subtle life force.

As they walk through the door, students are greeted by a tapestry of color and light, the energy of flowing, creative expression is palpable and real. Here gospel singers and blues musicians are at home with Buddhists, and a photograph of Osumi Sensei shares wall space with a painting of a giant alligator. In the middle of the room sits a vintage Steinway piano. The tones that emanate from its iron harp and seasoned wood chamber pierce the heart and satisfy the soul. Sound is made in the spirited way, announcing and delivering ecstatic currents of seiki. Like old spirit houses of the Caribbean and Brazil, and the oldest sanctified churches of the Deep South, music prepares everyone to work the spirit and take a ride on a train bound for the glorious heavens.

In this anointed space, the room can shape shift at any time, taking you to holy Kalahari ground where the Bushman sounds and vibratory motions are heard and felt. Or you can be transported to a traditional Japanese seiki jutsu clinic. The seiki stool that was given by Osumi Sensei sits in the room, near the piano, ready for someone to receive that style of transmission. All you know is that wherever you go in this class, it will soon change, taking you to another realm of vibratory experience. You might find yourself hearing the echoes of the St. Vincent Shakers of the Caribbean, as hands clap and voices shout while someone in the room shares her visionary journey to the spiritual classrooms.

From time to time, a volunteer sits on the seiki bench, ready for Brad and Hillary to give a session. This is no ordinary encounter. Movement takes place along with poetics, chant, and song. Anything can happen, from a healing to a blessing, guidance, awakening, or transmission. Perhaps the most amazing thing about such a session is how everyone in the room experiences it as meant for their own life. A grandmother shouts out, "I get it! We each volunteer to bring down a lesson for everyone else." "That's right," Hillary responds. Brad starts playing the piano and channeling a song: "Since you get it, now is the time to give it. Do you get it? If you give it, you get it. I see you caught it . . . everyone is catching on . . ."

When seiki fills the room and we are working the spirit, the session is for everyone. It appears that each member of the class is the perfect complement for all the other participants. No matter where you come from, no matter your beliefs or background, you bring a teaching that seiki helps bring out. We all celebrate and nurture one another. Here the true gift of sharing is found. When we help and celebrate another's entry into seiki, we also receive it.

A seiki community and network is being built, one movement at a time, hooking up all who belong to a long line of seiki practitioners. Dreams may personally introduce the visionary Kalahari, ancient Japan, and the Caribbean traditions, taking you to the spiritual classrooms where more mysteries are revealed and then shared. There is something magical and mysterious about this learning. Its bigness makes you humble as a tiny pebble. It is absorbed through the heart and felt in the soul, as it inspires mind and body to never stop moving. Words become free to be improvised as new lives are composed and played by seiki. A mentorship in seiki jutsu is nothing less than a tutelage in vital living, a never-ending spirited celebration of being alive inside eternity.

---

The only way to be mentored in seiki jutsu is to be repeatedly immersed in seiki. Here masters of seiki jutsu provide opportunities to experience awakened seiki, as well as help you avoid getting lost, pulling you back in when you get off track. Our mentorship in seiki jutsu is dedicated to promoting and advancing the wisdom of the world's oldest ways of spiritual healing and renewal—especially the Japanese art of handling the vital life force, the Bushman healing way, and the Caribbean mystical teachings regarding entry into visionary ecstatic classrooms.

With a small cohort of students, we meet to provide infusions of seiki and teach how to nurture it in everyday life. This includes supervision of the daily seiki jutsu exercise and the Bushman teachings of how seiki can deliver ecstatic spirituality. We also prepare our students for the spiritual classrooms, the visionary realm of transformative teaching and ordination. Through the study of the wisdom practices of diverse ecstatic spiritual traditions, we offer unique spiritual prescriptions for altering and enchanting everyday routines, incubation strategies for seeding spiritual dreaming, teachings in how to utilize and integrate ecstatic spirituality with significant relationships, and life force coaching in advanced seiki tuning. A mentorship in seiki jutsu provides multiple opportunities for healing, renewal, and guidance. We aim to help you become "spiritually cooked," as the Bushmen say, so that you may find your rope—your pathway—to God.

Seiki jutsu fosters spiritual growth and development in the broadest ecumenical spirit, open to any and all wisdom traditions from contemporary spirituality to ageless religion, literature, theatre, music, dance, comedy, and creative living. No matter what words you use to describe what you are looking for—whether it is spiritual awakening, soul renewal, creative revitalization, deep peace, meaningful personal growth, noteworthy self-improvement, existential enlightenment, everlasting bliss, holistic healing, significant transformation, or reinvention of your life—you cannot achieve it without a hookup to seiki. Furthermore, it is likely that you can't even know or articulate what you are truly looking for until you have been spiritually charged. A seiki jutsu mentorship provides an old-school way of "getting yourself right with God," in tune with the universe and prepared to initiate a remarkable life journey.

It wasn't that long ago that the practices of yoga, meditation, and acupuncture were relatively unknown outside of Asia. Now the reemergence of the non-subtle life force practice invites the world to know about the original transformative way, what first appeared on the mother continent of Africa. Now is the time for the resurgence of seiki. The whole natural cycle of healing and attunement includes both arousal and relaxation. Meditation and relaxation without spontaneous arousal and ecstatic expression is unnatural, as is movement that never rests. Many of us have been living as if only half of this equation is important. Whereas relaxation rests the mind and body, seiki wakes up spontaneous creative expression, tunes the whole being, and brings forth our relationship with divine mystery. With seiki, the relaxation response kicks in automatically when it is time for it to do so; after a peak surge of energized expression, the body moves effortlessly into relaxation. It's time for a holistic well-being practice that recognizes and honors both sides. Seiki jutsu holds the oldest wisdom that doesn't care whether you begin with silent stillness or loud activity. It knows that whatever the beginning is, it will change, doing so effortlessly and spontaneously. In this changing is found healing and revitalization.

Seiki practices around the world, from the Kalahari to the Caribbean, Bali, Japan, and elsewhere, teach that there are spiritual mysteries that can be brought forth by seiki. We address what we call "the twelve original mysteries" when mentoring others in seiki jutsu. The first of these mysteries concerns becoming tuned, which we have been discussing throughout this book. Here we find the secret to achieving well-being and inspiration for a fulfilled life, and anyone who sincerely practices a relationship with seiki will receive these benefits. For those who go deeper into seiki, other experiences may verge on the mystical. This is where we find the source of spirituality and profound wisdom teaching. Finally, the deepest immersions into seiki bring forth the highest transformative experiences possible. These are rare and available to those whose life purpose brings them to the spiritual classrooms, the source of all spiritual and transformative teaching.

We will now take a closer look at the mysteries that seiki can awaken in you, beginning with a review of how it tunes your whole being. It's important to recognize that the twelve original mysteries are not stages of consciousness or levels of achievement through which to measure spiritual progress. The more we indulge in that kind of categorical thinking, the farther from the heart of the mysteries we become. Know that it is enough to have a deep relationship with seiki, a love for God or the divine in your heart, and a sincere desire to be an empty vessel in service of something bigger than yourself. From there whatever your destiny is will arise naturally.

## THE TWELVE ORIGINAL MYSTERIES: GETTING TUNED

The first four original mysteries concern how to become tuned. If you are in tune, life plays beautiful music on you. The key to embracing vital living is to know how to tune your life. It has little to do with trying to move another step closer to becoming more spiritually developed with the aspiration of being liberated, actualized, or enlightened. Every morning we wake up with beginner's mind, and within hours—or minutes—are typically thrown off key, ushering in a breeze of irrational despair until we get retuned once again. Seiki helps bring forth natural, effortless, spontaneous tuning of the mind, body, and everyday routines.

The Bushmen do not regard any particular person as being spiritually enlightened. That very idea would send them to the ground convulsing with laughter. Instead, they regard every person as being equally capable of getting out of whack and falling out of tune. What matters to the Bushman way is knowing that we need to constantly retune ourselves, not just once a week but multiple times throughout the day. When you are in tune, you stand ready like a lighting rod to be hit by transformative lightning—openly available for seiki to fully charge and surge through you. When you are in tune and played by the gods, then and only then may it be said that you are spiritually awakened. In the Kalahari, you are a spiritually enlightened being, a healer, a teacher, and a wisdom keeper only in the moments when you are a tuned instrument for the gods to play. After each gig, you once again return to being a spiritual novice.

The first four original mysteries have to do with the ways in which seiki tunes your whole being.

First Original Mystery
## Spontaneous Movement
## Nurtures Health, Vitality, and Creativity

Spontaneous body movements nurture a sense of vitality that is inseparable from the flow of the vital life force. This, in turn, inspires health, creativity, and the enhancement of everyday life. It cannot be said enough that what is important are spontaneous, automatic movements rather than consciously driven choreographies. The original transformative practice is not to follow a scripted pattern, but to be spontaneously moved. It calls for improvised expression rather than memorized form. From the beginning of human culture, healers have encouraged the expression of body automatisms, particularly spirited trembling and spontaneous movement. This mystery alone is life changing and helps you have a connection with seiki that promotes health and optimal living. Everyone's well-being can be enhanced by the daily seiki exercise.

The practice of ecstatic dance takes a step toward spontaneous movement, but its practitioners must be careful not to conflate spontaneous movement with dance. Introducing categories of movement or rhythm (even when the performance of these is improvised) risks imposing frozen forms or theories that can interfere with seiki-inspired spontaneity. Seiki jutsu asks us to forget dance, even though seiki is always dancing us. It asks us to not interpret or distinguish forms that arise as a means of getting us ready to enact them.

Seiki is more than movement. It is even more than spontaneity. It matters little whether your hands are trembling or your whole body is rolling on the ground. Wilder movement is not necessarily evidence of more spontaneity or life force. Seiki is the unnameable vitality that never ceases changing. In the differences between anything that can be named, in the spaces between each note and each movement of the body, is found the life force of music, dance, and everyday living.

*Are you sitting in a lotus position trying to remain still, but feel a desire to wiggle or move? Listen to that voice, for it cares not what anyone else says. This inner voice is the teacher you have been waiting to meet: the wisdom of your whole body. If it asks to move, then allow it to move: bounce, wiggle, jiggle, jump, or not. Allow spontaneity to lead. Perhaps it will ask for a deeper stillness than your meditation teacher knows. Start a new spiritual revolution with a different kind of movement. Prepare to be an instrument for the expression of seiki. Get out of the way and allow the vital life force to lead you step by step inside your everyday.*

## Second Original Mystery
### *Heightened Tuning*

Whereas a general tuning first takes place with spontaneous movement, a heightened tuning kicks in when strong seiki inspires significant ecstatic experience. The natural and beneficial ways of performing highly aroused, spontaneous body movements began with the Bushmen of southern Africa, and then spread to the rest of the continent and throughout the African Diaspora to the Caribbean, Brazil, and the sanctified African American Church in the United States. Strong seiki or n/om inspires ecstatic spontaneous movement, creating a heightened tuning that readies you for spiritual experience.

Early African culture knew an intimate relationship with spontaneous experience, especially that which inspired enhanced seiki. There was no need to name and interpret particular movements as associated with different deities. Instead, movement was allowed to constantly move without any impositions of interpreted form.

Thousands of years later, first in China and then in Japan, after many ecstatic shamanic traditions had been quieted, Zen arrived on the scene to strip away the excessive verbiage in order to reveal the bare bones underneath. In that climate, the life force could again move spontaneously, less restricted by commentary, interpretation, naming, and form. Here seiki jutsu essentially brought back the n/om of our earliest ancestral culture.

*Forget any purposeful movement. If you are exercising effort to ecstatically dance, you aren't listening to seiki. If you force wild movements, seiki isn't present. If you scream and act out to convince yourself that you are full of the life force, then sit down and take a nap. You are more likely to receive seiki in a dream if your unconscious mind is set free. But dreams, as it is for being awake, are also constrained by all the assumptions you have about seiki, spirituality, and mastery. Throw away what you know, and allow deeper mind to move you into something you cannot bring about with the thought productions of shallow mind. Do not be concerned with which category of rhythm, Orisha, or geography of spirit is present. Be empty. Quiet the commentary and simply allow seiki to turn on your inner light and shine itself on a moving truth, one that changes its voice and metaphor to move the situation at hand. The less effort you exert, the more the vital life force can be present. The less knowing you impose, the more you will be filled by emptiness.*

*The most powerful movement of seiki takes place with a high frequency vibration that may not be perceptible to anyone observing. It can happen while you are sitting or lying down. An elder Japanese grandmother can hold more seiki than an Olympic athlete. The wisdom of seiki is found in highly tuned vibrations, not necessarily present or absent to an observing eye. Know this: you will know seiki when it arrives. It naturally stills the racing mind, bringing it back home to your body. Your heart will delight in feeling it and your soul will soar. If you question seiki, you have not experienced it. If you say too much about it, you are likely being tricked by your mind to think you know it, in order for mind's ceaseless discourse to remain in charge. If you truly know seiki you will own it, meaning you will "own the feeling for it." When you own seiki, you will start moving whenever you think about it or hear its name.*

*Move. Do not move. Be moved by the difference between movement and no movement. On the bridge of this difference is found a crossing into seiki, the wave that carries you back and forth across all polarities and dualisms. In these crossings are the movements that matter, as long as the movement never stops; except when it needs to stop, in order to move again.*

### Third Original Mystery
## *The Spontaneous Tuning of the Mind*

Seiki-charged talk helps tune the mind. When you are full of seiki, words and sounds may spontaneously come through you. Here there is no reliance on a script; your speech is as spontaneous as other body movements. As more seiki circulates through the ecstatic recipient, words give way to improvised sounds. The energetic voicing of sound is a higher level of communication than speaking in known semantics. As the ecstatic shakers of St. Vincent say, "Spiritual electricity can be shared with others when you feel and express this energy with your voice." In other words, seiki can be transmitted through sound.

Anyone who has witnessed an ecstatic Black church service is familiar with the "shouting" of a spiritually worked-up preacher. A master of seiki jutsu easily recognizes this as the voicing of seiki. If a preacher is not full of seiki (or to use their term for this source of energy, "holy spirit"), the performance feels inauthentic. It is an impersonated performance of seiki, rather than the real thing. Here the power of the preaching is found in the energy being transmitted rather than the interpretations of the text being discussed. Of course, a sacred text can contribute to awakening and feeding the life force, but it is the expressed vitality that touches people more than a rhetorical presentation of meaning.

The shouting of these preachers is a carryover from old African traditions long familiar with handling the vital life force. When a preacher is "sanctified," he holds the spirit within him and spirit speaks through his voice. Similarly, masters of seiki jutsu from Japan and masters of n/om in the African Kalahari voice seiki in order to transmit it to others. It is all the same. It matters not what inspires the awakening of the life force, though the poetic words of wisdom traditions, whether they speak of Jesus, Orishas, spirits, or beloved ancestors, meaningfully contribute to inspiring spirit's initiation and delivery. When it comes to being "anointed" with seiki it is the feeling evoked by the words, rather than any one particular belief system, that matters most.

One of the signs of an authentically awakened spiritual teacher and healer is that she voices seiki talk and sounds. This has been forgotten by cultures that have become disconnected from the art of handling seiki, n/om, chi, kundalini, the holy spirit, and the vital life force. As a consequence, in the guise of spiritual teaching many talking heads offer prefabricated platitudes and preformed routines without being ordained or anointed in any way by the vital life force. What we need are more "sanctified" recipients of seiki, whether they are preachers, singers, musicians, healers, spiritual teachers, or from any other position in life. Without seiki, there can only be deadbeat talk and inauthentic imitation.

The Guarani Indians of the lower basin Amazon in Paraguay, where Brad was also initiated, similarly believe that "word souls"—the talk of someone ecstatically aroused with the life force—are able to tune, heal, and inspire. This ecstatically inspired communication helps tune us and prepare a connection to receive heightened or enhanced seiki.

Whenever there is ecstatic experience, it will be reflected in speech and song. An energized voicing of seiki will arrive that may be more powerful and transformative than any body movement. Sometimes neither ecstatic dance nor the trembling hands of a healer can match the awakened seiki delivered through seiki-inspired talk or sanctified shouting and singing. Seiki jutsu brings back one of the strongest spiritual tools that has been all but forgotten in contemporary times—seiki-charged vocal expression. The technicians of vibrant ecstasy, seiki, n/om, sanctified holy ghost power, and the non-subtle life force have been too often ignored, minimized, and even ridiculed. Remember this: Any encounter with divinity will make you tremble with joy as you feel electricity surge through your whole being. Without a doubt, it will make you want to shout! Anything less is not a close encounter with seiki and holiness.

*We'd rather sing and shout about seiki than talk about singing and shouting. Don't practice making seiki-charged sounds; wait for seiki to stir up your voice. Or sing in a heartfelt way to bring on the seiki and share it with others. Tune and be tuned. Move in order to get a wheel turning. In its movement, creation is spun. As the spinning starts, feel a wind—a gentle breeze or a mighty storm. Like a ship at sea, allow your sails to carry you somewhere. Get on course, for the spirited whirl of holy wind will take you there. Seiki is the wind, you are the sail, and everything else, including you and seiki, is the sea.*

Fourth Original Mystery
## The Spontaneous Tuning of Daily Routines
Diverse healing traditions use some version of a "death and resurrection" ritual to existentially extinguish and bury everyday habits and patterns, making way for the birth of new forms of daily performance. This is another way of preparing the ground for spontaneous expression. For example, the Bushmen engage in the practice of "insulting the

meat," a way of teasing one another that helps free people from being overly attached to the interpretations and commentaries imposed by words, especially those that maintain rigidity.

When a Bushman hunter returns to the village with a big success, he will be proud of his achievement and people will celebrate the gift of meat. At the same time, the community will mercilessly tease him, perhaps suggesting that he sang a love song to his prey in order to sexually attract it. Any seriousness on the part of the hunter about his hunting skill is relaxed by humor, while at the same time he is honored in a way that implicitly acknowledges his skill. The hunter receives a gift from the community that enables him to have more wonder and awe about the mystery of hunting and not take it for granted. Here the hunter is softened and tenderized, made ready to be fed to the gods; this is to say that the community successfully hunted the hunter and offered him as meat. This is how Bushmen use words to create absurdity and humor that brings reversals, changes, and surprises in how we might be tempted to hold on to any singular, stuck meaning.

Seiki jutsu also encourages absurd teasing and humor to help precipitate more freedom of expression, along with a softening and loosening of our habits, thereby helping open the door for seiki to enter. It recognizes and utilizes the implicit wisdom found in unconventional approaches to psychotherapy, as exemplified by the legendary work of Dr. Milton H. Erickson. Here impoverished habits are deconstructed in creative ways, enabling an opportunity for the construction of more resourceful daily engagement. Through the prescription of irrational and absurd rituals and tasks, habits may be loosened as we tune ourselves for spontaneously generating fresh participation in everyday life. Seiki jutsu invites you to transform your life into an improvisational theatre, moving to a stage where more experimentalism in absurd performance is encouraged, whether at home, work, or play. Tinker, experiment, and invent changing ways of breathing more spontaneous life into your performance of yourself, doing so in order to attract and feed seiki.

*As Lewis Carroll hinted, whatever you do three times becomes true—that is, it becomes a habit structure that self-verifies itself with repetition. After three times, however, it starts becoming "false" (less authentically alive) as it loses its spontaneity and vitality over time. Seiki asks that you do one thing differently at least once a day. For example, you might say "jello" or "yellow" rather than "hello" to the first person you see at work. In addition to this daily task, repeat that newborn act for the second time—do it within a week—to experience how anything may become true. "Yellow, how are you today?" Finally, try something for the third time—do it within a month—so you can celebrate having found a truth. "Yellow, it's a nice sunny day, isn't it?" All that remains now is to undo whatever is performed more than three times, perhaps saying to yourself, "Hello, it's time to get mellow about this yellow."*

*In other words, the first action serves confusion, the subsequent reoccurrence feeds illusion, while the third time breeds conclusion. After that you have a habit that uncritically serves the maintenance of delusion. Do this experiment in undoing your everyday world, for it will help you know that getting ready for seiki requires ungluing whatever has been done, readying anything and everything to perform again for the very first time. Make sure you read these instructions three times before starting!*

*Though we speak of tuning the mind, body, and everyday routines, appreciate that these different names point to various entry points for transforming the same unity. Change your mind as your body changes the everyday. Transform the everyday as its body changes your mind. Alter the embodiment of everyday mind as its performance changes the way it indicates body, mind, and everyday. Think less about any of this and start feeling a change.*

*Celebrate the forthcoming change that has already been set in motion. This, in turn, helps change your changing, as creation is made more able to creatively create.*

## THE SEIKI LINES: GETTING ON TRACK

The next three mysteries regard remarkable mystical experiences that are able to come forth when you get on the "seiki line," "track," "rope," or "highway." Here you are carried further into the greater mysteries, but without a song you get nowhere—a song that touches you deeply is required for deeper entries into the vital life force. As Ray Charles soulfully sang the tune "Without a Song," "Without a song, the day would never end. Without a song, the road would never have been."

One of the greatest mysteries of seiki jutsu is that it awakens your singing voice. Even if you think you can't sing or have never sung in your life, once you have seiki you will be unable to stop singing—both inside yourself and out loud.

The original African masters of the vital life force utilized soulful music and its way of handling seiki. In fact, the n/om or seiki lines were regarded as songs, impossible to activate, feel, and travel on without singing. We have never met an ecstatic master of the non-subtle life force who does not appreciate the importance of bringing forth transformative sound. However, the contribution of music and rhythm to seiki was arguably not as fully developed in Japan as it was in African cultures. Here we see the most important teaching of the Bushmen. You can't have a strong seiki line, rope to God, or pathway to the most powerful healing practices without a song. We are talking about a song that lives in one's heart, ready to spring to life when feelings activate its heartfelt melody and pulse of life.

The earliest shamans were called the song catchers; without a song, there can be no authentic shaman. Traditionally in shamanic cultures, people fasted with the hope that they might receive a song. The music is more important than a vision. With a song, you get a seiki line, a road to spirit, and a spiritual tool that can energize and guide your life and help others. Without a song you have to fake it, follow someone else's routine, and go through the motions without the seiki-inspired emotions. In other words, without a song there is no enhanced vital life force. But when you receive a song, you own a seiki line that can lead to other mysteries.

Once you have a seiki line and are on track, it is as if an internal switch is turned on. Your body automatically takes over, knowing exactly what to do. An inner body pump is activated that results in the amplification of ecstatic experience that, in turn, brings forth the spontaneous know-how of healing and working the spirit. Being in tune brings you to the seiki lines, and once you get on track, the rest can follow without effort.

Of course, you have to stay on course with a seiki line and not be distracted by either worry or delight. If you get concerned about falling off track, you may indeed be thrown off track. Similarly, if you gloat about being in tune and on track, you can easily get tripped up. Getting on a seiki line requires staying on track. Any head trip dissociates you from being centered in your heart, where the music lies waiting to energize and reawaken. Let the heart steer without reflection, narration, or contemplation. It's the heart and its music that is the start button for getting things moving and keeping them moving in the right direction.

## Fifth Original Mystery
### Riding the Seiki Lines to Higher Mystical Experience

We cannot emphasize enough how nearly every indigenous healing tradition, including the oldest way of the Bushmen, teaches that one cannot be an ecstatic healer or wisdom keeper or enter the highest mysteries without music. The most important initiatory gift of a healer or shaman is receiving a song inspired by the mysterium tremendum. It provides a connection and pathway to the numinous. The higher realms of ecstatic experience are made more accessible through the emotional lift that heart-filled, inspired singing provides. If you meet someone who claims to spiritually teach or heal but does not have a song, walk away. You will know a master of the life force by how that person carries music. We are not talking about musical training, but authentic, seiki-inspired making of sound. You will feel its truth when you hear it. It can pierce you, transmitting seiki.

*Every human being who has become full of enhanced seiki can't stop hearing music and rhythm inside themselves. Typically, they also laugh easily and love the absurd. For sure, they don't take discourse very seriously. A true wisdom holder knows that the gods simply don't talk. They make music.*

*The highest vibrations of the vital life force automatically give rise to music. Here spirituality and music are the same; whenever trouble comes your way and makes you feel blue, the music is able to lift you up. Or if happiness blesses your day, the music is ready to play. It celebrates and elevates. Don't let your trickster mind convince you that it is otherwise. If a spiritual teaching doesn't awaken the music inside of you, then it has no seiki. If it's truly alive, music spontaneously comes forth and makes you want to move with delight, as seiki circulates freely and naturally shines the light. Music is the sign of whether spirit, holiness, and seiki (all names that point toward the same unnameable vitality of life) are present. You will know you have seiki when your life turns into a nonstop internal New Orleans second line, cabaret, or Broadway musical.*

*Both the Hare Krishna mantra and a sanctified gospel song share this common truth. Though they arise from different traditions, an infusion of their songs awakens spiritual consciousness. There is no need to gorge on words and textual interpretations. It's also not necessary to ingest mind-altering chemicals or plants. No reason to worry whether you should sit or stand in your practice, or eat raw tuna versus a steamed bean. Instead, align yourself*

*with the seiki lines. They will take you to the music that is capable*
*of piercing your heart and delivering a real-deal spiritual meal.*

Sixth Original Mystery

## *Awakening the Ecstatic Body Pump*

Bushman elders teach that there is a natural healing process within them that is activated by the ecstatic pumping movements of their abdominal area. It is believed to be the means by which sickness is pulled out of others and oneself. Surprisingly few healing traditions know about this ecstatic body pump. The Bushmen's ancient knowledge about these matters calls for an immediate reconsideration of our understanding and practice of healing. Bushman healers believe it is dangerous to attempt healing without mastery of this experiential ecstatic pump. The body pump not only helps pull the sickness out of the patient, it also pulls sickness and tiredness out of the healer. To not use it sets up the risk of taking in the other person's sickness. A healer should feel rejuvenated and healed after a healing; this is an indication that one is ready to heal others.

Even Japanese practitioners of seiki jutsu and other life force practitioners who do not ecstatically express sound and music are vulnerable to getting sick or having personal mishaps when they work with others. You should never lift the life force into the highest and most important frequencies without voicing a seiki-filled song. If there is no ecstatic sound making or if your voice does not come to life in a new way, do not attempt to heal anyone. You are not strong enough to do it without a song, no matter what your ego mind might say in order to convince you that you are ready.

*When seiki grabs hold of you, it can feel like it's making a tight*
*ball inside your belly. A force is then released that transforms your*

*whole being. In and out, contraction and expansion, inhalation and exhalation—this is the holy breath of the mystics. Not the air exchange through nose and mouth, but the pulse of seiki inside your inner furnace. This seiki breath is like a pump moving the vital life force up and down your spine, the seiki line that goes to your vocal cords. There songs are released. To get the seiki from the belly to the heart requires a song in the voice that helps pull it up. Now the pumping is everywhere—in the belly, heart, vocal cords, and the luminous cord above your head. When all this comes to life, the cord seems pulled by holy hands from up above. That's how it feels. Everything is pulsing and vibrating, contributing to the creation of sacred sound. The pulse and breath of seiki becomes a drum calling forth the music of the cosmos. In this seiki atmosphere, life is reborn and ready to heal.*

## Seventh Original Mystery
### *Becoming a Transmitter of N/om*

The strongest Bushman healers are said to be able to transmit n/om (or seiki) to others as a means of helping them become ecstatically awakened. This kind of transmission is also reported in the kundalini traditions and among other shamanic cultures with which we are familiar, including the Ojibway Midewin and Australian aboriginal medicine. Transmission of the life force is depicted by a variety of metaphors. For example, Bushmen talk about sending an "arrow," "nail," or "thorn" of n/om into another person. In the ecstatic traditions, teaching is largely about shooting arrows of n/om, instilling seiki, or transmitting the life force into an apprentice.

Hanging around a master of seiki jutsu helps prepare you to receive seiki. You are softened and seasoned by their teasing, absurdity, prescribed rituals, spontaneous movement, tactile interaction, seiki talk, and energized music. If the master has seiki, then don't worry about figuring out what you think you need to know. Allow seiki to work on you in the situations where a master can charge the immediate energetic atmosphere in a heightened way. Know that when you are ready, you will automatically start moving whenever seiki sounds are made. Soon seiki will come to you as you learn to minimize interpreting mind and release the music found inside your heart, or the "jukebox inside of you," as one elder sanctified parishioner called it.

*Someone is singing as seiki pulses through his voice. This sound holds a blessed energy, a vitality that can shoot an arrow of seiki into anyone whose heart is open to receive it. This is not the sound of everyday conversation. It is not anything like sleep-inducing hypnosis, or the calm voices heard at a contemplative wellness spa. The sound of seiki has a readily noticed change of frequency and is something that is strong and full of life. It can suddenly break into a shout, or the delivery of rhyme, improvised sound, or song, as it is unpredictable. Yet these sounds become deeply familiar when you are ready to receive seiki. It is the sound that calls you home to the vital life force.*

*The transmission of seiki embraces both inspired sound and movement. A spontaneous hand motion can itself release an arrow felt across the room. So can a sudden shift of the torso or an unexpected head tilt. The same holds true when a vibrating hand touches you or shakes your arm. The master of seiki jutsu is the bow, while seiki is the arrow. Mystery pulls back the bow and releases the arrow. Make yourself the target!*

## HIGHWAY TO HEAVEN: THE SEIKI LINE TO GOD

This set of original mysteries provides some of the most amazing mystical experiences that are possible for a human being. There is more to knowledge than what colleges and universities teach, including the schools of hard knocks and street smarts. There are virtual classrooms in the world of spirit, outside the range of radar and scientific measurement, where the profound transformative teachings are dispersed. When you are on the seiki line that the Bushmen call a "rope to God," you are led to these incredible classrooms. There the Bushmen healers learn more songs, dances, and ways of healing, where to find plants and animals, as well as instruction for the design of jewelry and fashion. In the Kalahari, the libraries, classrooms, lecture halls, laboratories, training grounds, workshops, initiation chambers, and performance stages are found in the visionary world of mystery. They are not physical structures but visioned places found in the world of spirit.

When you get this far along a seiki line, you not only receive the deepest and most transformative teachings, you are given a drink whenever you are spiritually thirsty. The so-called ancient golden elixir, or what the Bushmen call "God's water," is provided at those moments when you need a supercharge to move you further along. Here you soon find yourself no longer alone on the pilgrimage. You find others with whom to interact in transformative ways. Some are human and some are visionary. Together, you go further along the seiki superhighway to the greatest mysteries of spirituality.

After receiving a song, an inner pump, and a sacred drink, you are able to experience an incredible vibratory physical interaction with another person. As you move even further along the seiki line, the source of the deepest wisdom may open its door to a place in the spiritual universe that may be described as a kind of mystical library. Here you need no teacher—knowledge is simply downloaded and absorbed. Finally, if you stay on track inside your heart, the seiki line will take you straight to God's home. There you may be taught directly, even touched, by the Creator. This is the old way that follows the original path, the direct seiki line to God. There the original mysteries of the highest realm reside.

Eighth Original Mystery

## *Attending the Spiritual Classrooms*

Bushman healers and ecstatic teachers experience visionary travel to what they call "spiritual classrooms" where they receive specific guidance and instruction. The visionary ecstatic classrooms are sometimes described as visionary cities, underground places, mountain and sky regions, as well as unexpected encounters with a wide variety of idiosyncratic mystical presences. Cultural fasting rituals are often used to send one to a spiritual classroom. There visionary manifestations of seiki, or "spirits," are regarded as the teachers, whereas so-called human teachers or "pointers" make the preparations for visionary entry, pointing the way to particular classrooms. One of the most advanced ecstatic visionary cultures outside of the Kalahari Bushmen is the St. Vincent Shakers (see Keeney, *Shakers of St. Vincent*). Their elders teach that instruction from the spiritual classrooms is required for claiming any authority to speak about spiritual knowledge. The Bushmen believe this also. Enhanced seiki can open the seiki lines that carry you to the spiritual classrooms, an experience that is different from what active imagination invents during a guided fantasy or daydream. Here you enter something other than dream and fantasy. Again, you can't get to the spiritual classrooms without a song. Music is the high-octane energy that kicks things up a notch. You can't spiritually get home without it.

*There you are in a vision. Before you went to sleep, the vibrations of seiki cleansed the vessel and cleared out psychological residue and ego-projected fantasy, enabling mystery to call: "All aboard!" Whether you are taken to a spiritual airport, train station, port, or highway, someone will be there waiting for you, pointing the direction for you to follow. See all the seiki lines. The songs have transformed into luminous lines going in all directions. One of those lines is for you. A pointer will indicate which one is yours. Take a step toward it and find yourself immediately carried away,*

*flying along its path. In a few seconds it will transport you some-where. Do you have your passport to spiritually travel? Are you ready for seiki to take you to a classroom?*

*There is no spiritual anointment without a visit to one of these classrooms. There you are given the spiritual gifts, tools, instru-ments, and knowledge to carry out your assignment. You are given a purpose, mission, and task to bring back to the world. This is where you find your spiritual role in the grand scheme of things. It has always been this way and still is in places familiar with the seiki lines and the spiritual classrooms. Get ready for school. No matter how many spiritual books you've read or written, you don't spiritually know much of anything until you have been taken to this school. When seiki empties you, there is room for the universe to live inside of you, including the spiritual classrooms. In this vastness is found the wisdom of eternity. Infinite in its reach, seiki reaches out to say hello. As they say in St. Vincent, "Hello! Hello! Hello!" Seiki is knocking on your door.*

### Ninth Original Mystery
## *Drinking God's Water*

There are several ecstatic and mystical traditions that report a vision-ary experience of drinking a special elixir. Called the "golden elixir" by the Chinese Taoists, the Bushmen refer to it as "drinking God's water." This visionary fountain of life provides a multisensory embodiment of divine mystery. When one advances into the original mysteries, receiv-ing this elixir is one of the greatest gifts of spiritual renewal and deepen-ing. Masters of the non-subtle life force are familiar with this spiritual well. Among advanced practitioners of seiki jutsu, this water is taken as highly charged seiki and is sometimes called the "fountain of youth." Drinking seiki helps you feel young and is believed to inhibit the pro-cess of physical aging. It is not uncommon to hear Japanese practitioners comment about people who look much younger than they actually are: "They must have seiki."

*A man with a beard dressed in a long, flowing white robe is handing you a glass. At first glance it looks like a glass of milk, but as it comes closer you see it is a glass of light. It is time for you to drink seiki. As you swallow it, an incredibly warm feeling flows down the inside of your body, flowing from the top of your head to the bottom of your feet. It heats your insides and makes you tingle everywhere. You have been filled with seiki. Sometimes it can rise from the bottom of your feet and climb to the top of your head. No matter its direction, this drink always pours vitality throughout the whole of you.*

*Are you wondering, like others who drank this before, whether drinking this every day would bring immortality? It is seiki, after all, poured from the river of creation. The holy ones have given you a drink of eternity. The river now flows inside of you. Share it with others so the river flows from one to another. In this way seiki remains everlasting.*

### Tenth Original Mystery
## *The Experience of Vibratory Union*

The mystical experience of vibratory union through spontaneous movement takes place when two or more people, typically advanced practitioners of seiki jutsu, circulate seiki together. This enhanced seiki experience is an exhilarating ego-less form of relational interaction and is regarded as an advanced form of ecstatic teaching that opens the door to other spiritual mysteries. This kind of engagement is well known by the strongest shakers in Africa and was likely established thousands of years before Tantric practices began in the East. A heightened interactional experience of seiki between strong, thoroughly seasoned seiki masters is one of the most important forms of ecstatic transformation. Each person transmits seiki to the other at the same time, resulting in interacting waves of vibration whose harmonics trigger entries to further mystical experience.

*You are holding another person with whom you have a trusting and loving relationship, while both of you pulse at a high frequency. You aren't making this vibration happen, it just came to both of you spontaneously. To outside eyes, two people are hugging as they both tremble, shake, and quake. Inside the trembling, there are other orders of vibration that rise and fall. Crescendos provide a release and a return to another round of supercharging the dancing energy. Like a Tesla coil, electricity is climbing and shooting up a ladder. Up it goes until it hits the sky, sending lightning upward, only to return to Earth to start the process all over again.*

*You both continue building up this charge until you feel a "pop," a sound indicating that something has been released. You are separating from your physical body, as if shot like a cannon into the atmosphere. You go past the sky and enter the cosmos, speeding past the sun and stars, traveling all the way back to the beginning and ending of time. Through the vibratory union that holds the singular pulse of seiki, you are taken to the highest classrooms of human mystical experience.*

Eleventh Original Mystery
### Entering the "Mystical Library"
As you become more familiar with the supercharged seiki that is precipitated by interactionally sharing seiki, it will sometimes trigger a steady pulse within your spine that continues for twelve to twenty-four hours after the encounter. Later, during sleep, you might awaken to a

steady, high-frequency body vibration. This particular vibration is capable of opening an experiential entrance to what can be metaphorically described as a "mystical library," where visionary knowledge seems able to be directly downloaded. As one of the highest spiritual classrooms, the Bushmen believe that the old wisdom ways are brought back to life through this means of accessing wisdom through absorption. This is the ecstatic spiritual way in which ancient wisdom practices are conserved and passed on.

*You have pulsed inside the seiki embrace for hours; when you depart from one another, the unity of shared vibration remains alive inside. As you lie down to rest, you feel your spiritual body sliding out of yourself, entering a portal that reveals a large room, the largest room you have ever seen. There the holy books are found. They hold no words. Instead, they are filled with holy feelings. When examined they become songs that transform into seiki highways, connecting infinite varieties of endless spiritual knowledge. Welcome to the sacred universal library, the archive of all being. Here advanced spiritual wisdom teachings and gifts may be downloaded.*

*The more you receive, the less important your ego mind becomes. Learn how it is that the more powerful the vision, the simpler the revelation. There are no ego productions of inflation here. Only heart-piercing arrows of love are found on these shelves.*

*You are handed a book. "Open it up," a voice directs. As you open it, your heart is opened. You witness a single golden flower; bumblebees are flying around it. They turn into people dancing around a fire, singing and making themselves ready to bring the nectar of seiki to you. You have found the honey in the rock of ages, the sweetness that will forever change your life and never leave you standing alone wondering what it all means. You are now a poem, too complex to explain. Sing its lyrics and never*

*ever forget to say "thank you" with every breath, doing so until the end of time.*

## Twelfth Original Mystery
### *Climbing the Rope to God*

Bushman elders teach that the most important original mystery is visiting the Sky God in the "sky village." For the Bushmen, this access involves a mystical experience of climbing a rope that hangs from the visionary sky. It is believed that an experiential visit to the sky village, the highest spiritual classroom, results in significant personal renewal and preparation for the deepest and highest ecstatic work. It is an emotionally charged face-to-face, touching encounter with the ancestors and gods. For the Bushmen, this mystery—the ultimate mystery—is the seiki line that leads you to God.

*There it is before you. A rope is hanging directly from the sky, going all the way up to the heavens. This is more incredible than Jack's beanstalk or a skyscraper to the moon. It's a beam made of light, and it can become a ladder or a staircase, or even an elevator, whatever form helps you ease toward it. Take one step and up you go, smoothly gliding upward to the home of God. There a loved one from your past will meet you, perhaps a grandparent or long-gone friend. "Hold my hand," someone whispers. You are taken to the highest place, the place where the holy ones reside. There anything can happen.*

*This is the rarest experience for a human being, more important than climbing Mount Everest or winning the Nobel Prize. Honor anyone who has gone into the heavens and come back to tell you about it. Each time a person goes up, he goes up for everyone. Jacob climbed this holy ladder, as have some Kalahari Bushmen healers and St. Vincent shakers. Somewhere near you, long ago, a sanctified practitioner saw the rope to God. She climbed it for you. When you fully realize this, you will feel an emotional lift, perhaps feeling as though you have been physically lifted off the ground. You have been raised, for this is how others pull us up the ladder, staircase, and rope. If you feel it, you will notice that a song is coming forth. That song can pull you up even further. That song has a hold on me. "I sing because I'm happy. I sing because I'm free."*

Over the last forty years, Brad has experienced the original mysteries described in this chapter and has spent thousands of hours discussing them with spiritual elders from the Kalahari to the Amazon. Among other things, he drank mystical water, experienced transformation into other experiential realities with other shamans, visited the library of mystery, transmitted seiki, and traveled the seiki line to God. When Hillary joined Brad in their work as healers, her immersion in seiki brought forth her own experiences of many of the original mysteries described here, including receiving a song and visits to the spiritual classrooms. These experiences are what soften us, prepare us to work with others, and keep us inside the seiki current.

It is important to realize that everything is loosened, freed, and shaken up by the spontaneous entry of seiki, including your ideas, beliefs, ways of knowing, and spiritual practice. In other words, seiki deconstructs, deprograms, empties, clears, cleanses, and readies you to make room for the original mysteries. Seiki jutsu radically challenges any understanding of shamanism, healing, spirituality, creativity, art, dance, music, and even what constitutes mind, body, soul, ecstatic experience, love, and divinity. By its very improvisational and spontaneous nature, seiki can never be tamed or conceptually boxed. It is off any conceptual grid.

A mentorship in seiki jutsu teaches that seiki moves on its own accord and is more likely to surge through you when you are empty of categorical thinking, demanding purpose, and selfish expectation. It requires that you be willing to have an ever-expanding and childlike openness, be comfortable with apparent contradictions, express new-found creativity, encourage unexpected silliness, and nurture the wisdom to appreciate mistakes. Seiki is better served by paradoxical and absurd expression. Get ready for seiki by shocking your personality, messing with your ego, teasing know-it-all mind, tossing your beliefs around, and tripping over every previously unexamined assumption. If you persevere, you will learn to love being moved for no reason at all other than feeling totally alive.

You must lose everything to find the nothing that is really something. Encourage love rather than power. Be kind and gentle. Play and open your heart to the delight of being fully alive in the moment. Be unready for seiki to dance you. For god's sake, do not get too serious about any of this. At the same time, take this absurd advice as if your life depended upon it.

Get ready for receiving seiki by hanging out with it. Jump into its flowing river and be anointed by its current. Seiki jutsu hosts the original way of transforming the human body, mind, heart, and soul. We mentor others in seiki jutsu in the same way that the Bushmen metaphorically describe the way they mentor: "You are thrown into God's pot and cooked."

Many cultural traditions have found their way to seiki, doing so with a deep love that permeates its celebrative spirituality. Wherever seiki is found, it stages an experimental concert of ecstatic spontaneity. Seiki jutsu is more than healing and spirituality, renewal, and well-being. It is the modus operandi for expressing whatever the creative life force is ready to perform.

The history of how people have related to seiki (see Keeney, *Shaking Medicine*) can be seen as an ongoing spiritual performance experiment. In our teaching and practice, we emphasize the ancient ecstatic know-how of the Kalahari Bushmen, the bare bones knowing of Japanese-inspired seiki jutsu, the spirited expertise of the Caribbean in matters concerning the spiritual classrooms, and the praise-oriented music of

the old-school sanctified African American church. In this highly seasoned spiritual gumbo, transformative experiences of all natures are *Changes*
called forth: changes of body, changes of heart, changes of mind, and
changes of soul.

Rather than talking about change, seiki serves bringing it forth.
Here anything can happen. In our public work, lightbulbs have
exploded, fire alarms have gone off, speakers have disintegrated, micro-
phones have caught fire, and lightning has struck the building. More
importantly, people have experienced radical transformations and found
themselves filled with ecstatic delight, expansive love, and unstoppable
creativity.

Are you wondering what the next step is for you? We suggest this
immediate task, a ritual for getting started. Write the following sentence on the first page of this book: *I want seiki.*

Place the book in your freezer, but take it out to thaw before you
go to sleep. Imagine that the specially made request sends a message to
seiki, doing so through the deepest processes of your unconscious mind
that spring forth during your sleep. Each morning when you wake up,
write another request in the book, doing so on the next page. Make a
slight change in what is written, such as *"I really want seiki." "I truly
want seiki." "I mean it, I am asking as sincerely as I can for seiki." "Please
bring me seiki." "I'd love to receive seiki." "My life needs seiki, and I am
hoping it will come." "I am asking for seiki and believe it will be delivered."* Do this every day, writing down an altered request for seiki on
each new page, placing it in the freezer, and taking it out to thaw when
you sleep.

You will know that something is happening with seiki when you
feel a new wonder, creativity, and vitality in your life. Your intuition will
start to unthaw, suggesting what you might do next. You don't have to
understand anything; it is better if you don't. Instead, wait for a feeling,
intuition, or excitement to thaw inside of you. Do not stop communi-
cating with seiki. Do anything to make your messages noticed. Stand
on your bed and read what you have written. Write your request in a

foreign language or use the Morse code. Or better yet, sing it. Dance it. Shout it. Drop one tear on what you write in the book. Or tell your request a joke. Do anything at all, especially if it arises spontaneously. Why not cover your request with a colored piece of cloth. Dress it up. Adorn it. Name your request. Give it a symbol. Write it with both hands. How about a different color for each letter? Mirror writing? Write it sitting, standing, lying down, or in a yoga posture. Take the book to a holy place and write it there. Write each word of your request at a different location. There is no end to how you can ask for seiki.

If you persist and are sincere, we assure you that something will happen. Seiki will show up at your front door. Make sure you are listening for it. Get ready to welcome seiki to your home and everyday life. Enjoy your first steps toward seiki and the mysteries that stand ready to take you on the ride of a lifetime. We sincerely want you to receive seiki, knowing that it wants you as much as you want it. Court it, and woo it. Convince seiki that you want it in your life. That's the best way to advance toward what you most truly desire!

# 8

# HATCHING
# A SPIRITUAL UNIVERSE

Seiki delivers more than cheap talk. Tune out the platitudinous spiritual chatter and instead tune in to the soul-stirring rhythmic pulse of seiki. We again invite you to follow some old school advice and pay more attention to whoever sings and moves spontaneously whenever holy things are mentioned. Be not concerned whether they are professionally trained, are musically in tune, or can do little more than raise their arms. Feel the heart and soul carried by their sound and movement. You can hide inside talk, but you can't lie when your heart inspires you to sing and move.

It's time to feel the seiki lines, hear the sanctified music, drink a glass of the vital life force, visit the spiritual classrooms, climb the ropes to God, and find out about the original mysteries that have been present since the first human beings opened their hearts to seiki. Let us return to what has always been available, even before the great religions were born and the holiest books were written. The original mysteries are the foundation of vibrant spirituality. Let us start at the beginning when mystery had its say and people followed its way.

In the beginning, God's egg cracked and a universe was born.

---

When you first fall in love, whether it's with a partner or your newborn child, you receive a hint about the ultimate secret to the cosmos. From that moment on, like everyone else you set out on a lifetime pilgrimage that takes you from one moment of love to another, finding different kinds of heart-to-heart connections along the way. If you are lucky, you eventually arrive at the holy grail. There you discover that there is only one teaching, though it can be expressed in many different ways: *You were born to long for love, and in the longing is found the fullest living.* The energy that pulls you when you long and love is seiki, the vital life force.

The Portuguese word for longing is *suadade.* Though suadade is typically associated with the longing for the presence of a departed loved one, there is more to it than that. Whenever there is deep love, we cannot stop longing for the other even when that person is by our side. This longing for complete union is the ache of love's pulling. We feel suadade for those we love both past and present, as well as those who are real or imagined. It may also be a longing for that which is not even consciously identified. The deepest longing inspires and opens ecstatic entries to the miracles and mysteries of life brought forth through our journey in search of the absolute fulfillment of love. We love with longing, and our longing is the howling, praising, singing, and dancing of love. Love moves in circles, as it never stops chasing itself. Suadade makes the world go round, like a mythological dragon that circularly chases its own tail as it stirs a mighty wind and breathes the fire of life's vitality. This wind and fire is seiki, the non-subtle life force.

*When you are full of seiki, there is no need to consider any evolution of consciousness, progression of spirituality through stages of development, or pilgrim's journey to the Kalahari, Tibet, Boulder, Sedona, California, or any points along the way. The spiritual cosmos exists in the felt rhythm, pulse, and heartbeat of eternity. Its journey is circular, bringing you home to love.*

Love is complex; true love holds many contradictions. Whether love is fulfilled or unfulfilled, it breaks our hearts wide open. Finding your love can hurt as much as losing it. Love holds both agonizing pain and liberating joy. Suffering and happiness are necessarily wed in matters of love—they are both found inside the contrary but complementary embrace of life and death.

Your life is a quest for love, and you are pulled and moved by your longing for it. When the pulling of love breaks your heart wide open, the cosmic egg is cracked. Get out of the way and allow God to break open your heart. This is when you hatch the spiritual cosmos, a divine holy ground where love rules supreme. Here you are filled with seiki and find a homecoming for your searching heart. Only then is your hunger satisfied and your deepest thirst quenched.

In the greatest mysteries of human experience, especially those that involve the divine, sacred, and spiritual, love is always present. When we say that we long for God's love, it is another way of expressing our biggest, deepest, and most important yearning. With the Bushmen, we sing because we are happy that the source of life's vitality, seiki, is found in the longing, pulling, and feeling of God's love.

We want you to hatch the spiritual cosmos and give birth to this immense love that no category can hold. Do so with the belief that this is possible if and only if you proceed boldly, creatively, and wholeheartedly.

The first teaching about spiritual "hatching" originated in the Kalahari, where the few remaining Bushman spiritual elders still even know about it. The Bushmen say that, though it is a rare occurrence, from time to time the Creator of Creation delivers an extraordinary sacred egg to those whose hearts are ready to crack open and receive an infusion of a miraculous, unfiltered divine love. This luminous egg, called "God's ostrich egg" by our first Kalahari ancestors, was typically seen as standing the same height as an adult human being. The only teachers who may authoritatively speak of the egg are those who have received it and live inside its infinite luminosity. Whatever is true in any religion or spiritual teaching was hatched from this egg, or from the luminous rays it projected into the world; everything from the divine cosmos is found inside its shell.

In the whirling of the infinite unknowable, there is a constant movement of change that can never be stilled or understood. It is not for minds to hold, but for hearts to feel. The heart of God pulls as your heart longs to experience this pulling. When love knocks on your door, the pulling awaits. When love's arrows pierce your heart, the pulling comes further inside. In all matters of love—big and small—the movement of pulling and longing draws you nearer to the heart of God. It is this motion that gives birth to the non-Newtonian law of ecstatic emotion as it rides the tides of the spiritual ocean, creates healing potion, and is worthy of loving devotion.

*The hatching of the light begins with a sense of light-headedness. You feel free of worry and burden. Lightness and euphoria spread throughout your body, and gravity seems to disappear as you become almost weightless. There is no resistance, no friction, nothing to stop your movement and destined flight. You glide rather than walk, ready for the pulling to carry you forward. There is no knowing that is separate from the fullest presence inside this movement. Yet there is a sense of all knowing, as you realize that whatever is asked will*

*pull forth its answer effortlessly and completely in a way that does not surprise, but seems the way it should have been surmised.*

*Now the pulling completely has a hold on you. It guides you to a holy place, perhaps a Gothic stone structure with diffuse light and stained glass windows. You sit down in the front pew. There you feel a tremendous awakening inside your body. A fire ignites at the base of your spine. At the same time a tightening takes place within your belly. It feels like a knot the size of a fist has formed there. As it tightens the fire gets hotter. Without notice the fist begins to contract and then release. It has become a pump, and it is lifting the fire up your spine.*

*Slowly and surely it climbs, bringing with it the certainty that this experience is the destiny of your life. None of this feels scary or weird, no matter how it may sound when it is later spoken and written about. It is the most natural thing that could be taking place for you right now. At the same time, there is no doubt that this is the most powerful experience a human being can have and that it will be forever life changing. Although it seems like something greater than nuclear power is moving inside your body, you are paradoxically feeling more tender, soft, and relational. You only feel love—for everything and everyone. Not the love of romance novels or preachy feel-good sermons. This love feels like the strongest current of life itself. It is the stream of life's essence pouring through you, and it is a holy thing. There is absolutely no doubt about it: You have entered and dissolved into the current of the great cosmic flow. You are inside the vessels of God.*

*When the ball of fire was first lit, your heart began to expand and continued to expand as the fire ascended. Your reach now grows far beyond that of your physical self. You feel a blazing heat and energy permeate through every cell. All of this takes place as your body trembles and shakes. In an instant you know why there were religious groups called "Shakers" and "Quakers." In this kind of rapture, shaking happens automatically. Again, it feels natural.*

*There is nothing strange about it. It is as natural as breathing.
The shaking vibrations are transforming you in some indescribable and mysterious way. This is the world of seiki.*

We wish we could say that every human being is able to stand in front of this egg, but that would not be telling the truth. Few people are chosen to witness God's luminous egg in a face-to-face encounter. Why they are chosen, no one knows. But when it happens to someone among the Bushmen, the whole community celebrates, because any spiritual gift given to one person is a gift given to all. The Bushmen say that the person who experiences God's egg is one of the lucky ones. They are specially chosen spiritual teachers because what they teach comes through the direct illumination of the divine.

Those who face the divine egg of illumination and receive the calling to transmit its vital force find that the wisdom teachings are directly downloaded into them. Facing that egg in an ecstatic state, they experience the holy ones who have walked before them. They will recognize some but not all of these teachers. The teachers will include the Buddha, Jesus of Nazareth, the Virgin Mary—on and on the list goes, as the parade of luminaries traverses through culture, space, and time. Not only are these images seen in the light of the egg, they are felt in your heart. You tremble more with the joy and love that this transmission involves. This is the way the making of an ecstatically illumined healer, shaman, and spiritual teacher takes place.

Again, we are aware that words alone cannot convey these truths. Feelings of this life-giving and life-changing love hold the truth, and the feelings we have as we write are what we hope will cross the text-to-heart divide. Our hearts want you to feel the truth behind this statement: You must find your special longed-for destiny, the path of loving that is uniquely yours. It is the holiest road for you to follow. Whatever its form, it is part of the greater interstate network of love, the pathways that pull us as we long to come home inside the heart of God.

*We pray that you might enter a capillary of the divine, flow into its streams and river ways, becoming a part of the holy sea. There the waves never stop moving—rising and lowering, back and forth—as the sea pulses with the pulling and longing of creation's love for what it is always creating. Though you consist of mostly water, spiritually you exist as less than mist—such is the teaching of mystery. Become the carrier of the invisible motion that binds every molecule of holy water. Let others ridicule, while you carry the wisdom of the anointed fool, moving on a seiki stool, riding a spirit mule, attending mystery school, and entering the depths of the sacred pool.*

Though few will face God's egg directly, it brings a teaching that is true for everyone's life. A special hatching must take place in order for you to step into your ordained destiny. This destiny is first and foremost to becoming a pilgrim of the heart, a warrior for sacred love, and a spirited deliverer of all the ways your heart desires to celebrate the longing that pulls you forward into expressing the ecstatic divine. There is a unique prescription that can help you become reborn through hatching the spiritual cosmos for your life.

We invite you to begin your journey tonight! On a fresh piece of paper—perhaps red paper to honor the spiritual heart—draw yourself an oval egg. Make it approximately the size of your hand. Now cut out the paper egg with a pair of scissors, and with a pen draw a crack down its middle. Make the crack look jagged, like a lightning bolt. Hatching a spiritual cosmos has the electrifying impact of spiritual lightning. It will bring a bolt and jolt of seiki to energize your newfound life.

Hold this egg over your heart every night while lying in bed, just before you go to sleep. Think of the luminous egg that comes to every spiritual teacher whom God has chosen to pass on this knowledge.

Know that there is also an egg that is specially designed for you. Your egg was given to you at birth. You need to hatch it so your truest self and life purpose can be known. As you hold the egg over your heart, let your sincere longing and childlike excitement send ripples of seiki through your body. Ask the egg to hatch as you sleep. Mention that it would be nice if you could see it hatching in your dreams, but that you trust the gods to decide whether they want you to see this taking place. Accept that it is going to take place.

Finally, sing the egg a bedtime song—any song you would sing to a child to help her go to sleep at night. You can sing it silently, but it is better if you sing it out loud. Sing it with all your heart and know that the gods listen to anyone who does not hold back authentic emotions of love and longing. This is most important: You must voice unconstrained sincerity. Then place the egg underneath your pillow and sleep on it.

Do this every night for the next seven nights or longer, and believe that this is the time in your life when you will hatch the spiritual cosmos into your life. Inside this new reality will be your second life, your newborn presence in the ways of spirited love. Think of this throughout each day, and do everything you can to flood your consciousness with this realization. Write notes to yourself that say things like, "A new cosmos is coming," "I will soon be a new kind of loving presence," "The hatch is opening," and "A new birthday is in the making."

You may have a vision or dream of your egg hatching, or you may wake up in the morning feeling different, even though you don't remember what happened in the night. Make a commitment to sleep with this egg for at least one week, the amount of time it took for God to create the world. You might hatch the cosmos during the first night, or you may wonder whether it happened later in the week. If you do this sincerely, something will get hatched.

As you prepare to hatch the egg, imagine that in some spiritual realm your guardian angel (and ancestors) will also be doing the same. Your guardian angel will be sleeping on her egg, praying that you will hatch yours in order to help her hatch her own. Yes, she is feeling the fire in her belly while spiritual lightning has entered her heart. She is doing this for you because she, like all other spiritual servants, sacrifices herself so you may receive the spiritual treasure. The ball of fire is moving up her spine as she trembles and shakes. She sings and wonders what song you will sing to your egg tonight. She is in this all the way with you, as are the Bushman ancestors in the sky and the gods who first invented love and your capacity to long for it.

What a beautiful cosmos love can create. It asks you to participate in its ongoing creation. Love wants you to stretch the cosmos further, making more room for the infinite joy it wants to share. In the clouds are the tears of joy and suffering that the gods pour on us so that all things may grow, including the capacities of hearts to long for the stars in the evening sky.

When one person receives God's luminous egg, we all are given its gifts. But we must ask for this hatching in a way that involves more than words. Demonstrate to the deepest parts of your being and the highest beings of the heavens that you sincerely want to hatch the cosmos. When your sincere request is seen, heard, and felt by the gods, the new birth will begin. It was never about how much you knew or how much you deserved any of this. It is simply about sincerely asking. Ask and you shall receive. Knock and the door will open. Place the egg underneath your pillow and the cosmos will hatch with a newborn you inside it.

As the luminous egg shines its holy light on the beholder, the ancient ones shoot arrows of love into the hearts of those who ask for illumination. With the arrow is a song that pierces the heart. The songs hold and express the great longing and enable the pulling to move us into the depths and heights of the holy. The egg is ready to hatch. The spiritual cosmos is ready to be born. All that waits is your making an egg and preparing yourself to sincerely sleep on it in the night. This is how the gods have asked you to procreate the heavens. There is no need for any other magic. The longing must be expressed in the sincere asking. The deepest part of you must hear and feel your voice. This is how the gods tell you that you have been heard. Speak and sing to yourself so you may know the gods are listening.

Into the light of the night, the twilight of spirit, you must go. There is the place for giving birth to the holy presence of divine light. You must ask not only for yourself, but for others who are longing for the truth of God's biggest love. Do it for them because they can't make it without you. Similarly, they are doing it for you. Together we can enter the heavens. Alone we are grounded without flight.

Find another person to do this hatching with. It can be your spouse or friend. It can be someone to whom you spontaneously introduce yourself, and if you strike up a warm conversation and connection, ask that person to participate in a spiritual experiment with you. Whoever you find, each of you must send words of encouragement to the other throughout each day during the full week of hatching. Text your partner with words that say, "I am visualizing that you are hatching the cosmos," "I feel that you will create a new world," "This week is the beginning of a new life," "Together we can accomplish anything," "I want you to find the love of your longing," or with a smile, say, "We are on a mission for God."

It is never too late to find true love. Somewhere out there is your soul mate, your perfect partner in the longing and the living. This person may already be living with you, though the two of you have not yet been hatched. The other person you desire may be your guardian angel who already lives in the spiritual cosmos waiting for you to come home. The world of God's love is mysterious and it rarely makes sense, but it is always present and true. You were born to love. Now it is time for you to love in order to be born.

In the egg lives the divine heart. It beats the rhythm of longing, the breath of living. It wants to come out and play in your everyday. Stop waiting to love. Do not delay fully living anymore. Say yes to love so it may pull you across to the other side, the place where poets long for the words that open hearts. You are here to be a lover, an extreme devotee of love that has no limits and is beyond measure. This is your time to love.

You are forever more to think of your bed as a nest. There you may hatch eggs of love that give birth to the loving cosmos. In the holy light of dream night, the teachings are given. Join the original ancestors—the saints, angels, prophets, poets, musicians, and lovers of love who are doing everything they can to bring you over. In the twilight you will find the crack that opens the sky. The luminous egg is calling your name. It is singing for you, pulling on your heart. "Come home, come home. Ye who are weary come home." There in the light of love is a baptism of rebirth and renewal. It is time for you to be a child who can pass through the gates of heaven, the spiritual cosmos for all who are lost and waiting to be found by love.

When the spiritual cosmos is hatched, seiki pours into you. No matter the name of your role in life, your mission is the same as every other human being who has received seiki. You are to become a rain-maker, bringing seiki to a world that is dry and arid, desperate for a drink of holy water that has been fetched from the seiki stream. Fill yourself with this water and be a living well. This is what it spiritually means to achieve well-being.

>*Seiki comes to deliver the water*
>*Rocking you like a teeter-totter.*

>*Flooding away the understood*
>*Empty mind is very good.*
>*Become the rain that eases pain,*
>*As thunder's belly laughs away blunder.*

>*Then shine your light upon tender ground*
>*The morning dew of life now found.*

# A CONVERSATION ON JUGGLING ZEN, JAZZ, AND SEIKI

Seiki jutsu arguably enters the experiential territory of a liberated Zen roshi when it strictly attends to what spontaneously arises in the here-and-now, doing so free of attachment to any narrative or habit of interpretation. In its purest form, Zen loses the discourse of Zen and the seiki practitioner loses any distinction or duality between what it is and isn't. In the case of Osumi Sensei, though she was licensed as a body-worker, she was never conscious of being primarily organized by such a role. She simply was full of seiki and responsive to its calling in every situation that asked her to participate in a transformative way. The same is true of any practitioner who gives authority to the importance of the vital life force. As the Bushmen say, they become someone who lives for and hunts for n/om. People filled with seiki search for it in every aspect of life. When seiki or n/om circulates freely inside, there is only seiki dancing with those who encounter it, whether this is oneself or an interaction with others. Therapists, counselors, coaches, bodywork-ers, ministers, teachers, engineers, musicians, poets, and artists, among others, who are filled with seiki become improvisational artists dancing with life's creative vitality.

Here we offer a conversation that discusses the relationship between what we propose are the three ingredients of a spiritually awakened life: Zen, jazz, and seiki. The art of living with the non-subtle life force requires that all these continuously bring forth one another in a never-ending juggle. Go ahead and throw them in the air until you catch the art of juggling yourself. In this circulation of movement is found seiki jutsu.

**BRAD TO HILLARY:** I like the way you describe awakened ecstatic living as an interplay of three domains—bare bones knowing, improvisational expression, and the nurturance of seiki. Can you tell us more about that?

**HILLARY:** As you become more filled with seiki, there is less to say and know. Even saying "bare bones knowing" may give the erroneous impression that there are root concepts or essential ideas that need to be discovered and dug up. When I say "bare bones" I mean we can strip everything away and see the skeleton frames built by mind. Now watch those bones turn to dust. Or better yet, become filled with seiki and make those bare bones dance! Zen is a dancing mind and a moving body. Seiki will hear the drumming of your heart and flow right in. Be moved and discover you are jazz. As you improvise yourself into forgetting that you are improvising, you may express anything and everything. You speak for the falling leaf and the moving tide. Zen, jazz, and seiki are the only things you need to embody—the three aspects of being fully alive.

**BRAD:** You must strive to realize them all. The good news is that when you step fully into one, you find yourself inside the others. Zen, jazz, and seiki are like three doorways into the same always-changing unity. Know, however, that it is impossible to fully realize any single one. Laugh at the idea of spiritual mastery, and then seek mastery anyway. Through your efforts, you will learn how to utilize the unknowable that holds all situations. Doing so carries you deeper into respecting the absurdity of thought and deed. This deep realization must be earned, rather than learned, by blood, sweat, and tears. As you dive into these existential depths, you ripen your being and are able to rise again and again, becoming ready for another plunge.

HILLARY: The more mysteries we experience, the more we learn that there is only one mystery. Life is the mystery, all of its simplicity and complexity, and all of its movements, transformations, and changes. The vitality of life, the "life of life," is seiki.

BRAD: The life stream is always flowing even when we forget that it is. As others have said before us, the best learning is an unlearning of the habits that resist the natural flow. As Michelangelo released the design already present in stone, we must release the movements already taking place in our frozen states.

HILLARY: Should we tell our students that meditation is always a moving meditation? There's no such thing as stillness.

BRAD: Perhaps we should place a microphone on their hearts and bellies so they can hear all the motion and commotion that is going on inside. Everything is changing, moving, and singing, both inside and outside of us.

HILLARY: Be still in order to experience movement. Move in order to experience stillness.

BRAD: Yes, movement and stillness are dancing together; this is the movement holding both.

HILLARY: As I sit, I feel a current of seiki arise within.

BRAD: I'm with you as we hold hands. There is a rolling wave inside that constantly changes form. It can be one large wave that rises from the base of the spine to the throat, or it can break into tinier trembles that flow in different directions. A bolt of electricity can ripple across our chests, rocking each shoulder. This is a meditation that moves, absorbed in the rock and roll of seiki, becoming the never-ending arrival and departure of differences that ambulate and modulate into shifting forms.

**HILLARY:** Seiki moves us back and forth across the border between that which is always changing and the temporary forms that change creates. We are waves whose meetings are moving, moments that begin, end, and then meet all over again.

**BRAD:** Perhaps our teaching should be expressed in a way that unravels whatever it is we say, as we say it, and then brings it back to itself. Since there is only movement, everything is moving, including these statements. In other words, what can be said must change as soon as it is said, or else the movement being pointed to gets lost.

**HILLARY:** Even that must move, for spontaneity needs no sidebar commentary. It just happens, including when it is not happening.

**BRAD:** In the shifting expressions a bridge is crossed. That bridge is relationship and the crossing carries the interactions, the dancing that brings us forth.

**HILLARY:** Seiki needs no explanation. Nor does any mystery, including love.

**BRAD:** What are we to say if there is nothing to say?

**HILLARY:** As long as our words are held as play, or as letters written on the sand free to be blown away, then we can feel free to give voice to whatever moves us.

**BRAD:** We can't emphasize enough how important it is to wake up the music inside you. We all need to switch on the inner jukebox. Without it you can't catch the most important ecstatic feeling, the holy tidal wave that carries you into holiness and a love bigger than Cupid ever imagined.

**HILLARY:** Everything is holy, even when you are lost and not riding the wave, even when you fall off the seiki line. The truth is, you are always living inside the rope to God, traveling on the seiki highway.

**BRAD:** Say Amen, Somebody!

**HILLARY:** You have to get lost to find the spirit. Step right up and take a ride, find the end of time. Get yourself on that train, before and after the spiritual rain.

**BRAD:** Seiki loves words even if they are absurd. Seiki loves keeping emotions real. That's why it can serve a well-balanced spiritual meal.

**HILLARY:** Some of the folks we know who are masters of seiki never heard of the word "seiki." They talk about n/om or the holy spirit. Or they say nothing at all about it. They are it. Those old country sanctified churches that are getting harder to find implicitly know about the seiki exercise. They call it a holy ghost party.

**BRAD:** I wish we could send a holy lightning bolt out of this book right now. Imagine if the ink on this page started wiggling and then turning to liquid. As it drained off the page it suddenly condensed itself into a line, stood up, and shot itself into the reader's heart. Without warning, a song arises. This is what the wave of holiness is capable of bringing. Remember when we thought about hosting our own storefront holiness church, delivering seiki inside the music and poetry of sanctified services?

**HILLARY:** We did do that, but that's another story. Suffice it to say that there are too many Christians who pay more attention to arguing about the words, even claiming to be spokespersons for "the word." Actually it's not just the Christians. There are fundamentalist Buddhists, fundamentalist atheists, fundamentalist psychologists, fundamentalist vegetarians, and so on. I bet there are even fundamentalist anti-fundamentalists. It's a human trap to which no one is permanently immune. That's why we must be continuously shaken by seiki! The gods are at the highest bar, ready to serve us a life-force martini.

**BRAD:** Too many people haven't yet found their inner jukebox. When I see Christians shouting angrily on the street corners, I sometimes ask them to sing a song about their love for Jesus. They act like they never heard of music, which I take to mean that they haven't met Jesus.

**HILLARY:** You should sing to them instead.

**BRAD:** Or let's get a bunch of our friends to dress like George Harrison and sing Hare Krishna. Serve a love feast to the word beasts.

**HILLARY:** As long as it's foolish enough. As you reminded me, you have to be a "fool for God." I still enjoy hearing about the time you went to a religious college when you were 18 years old and started your own newsletter called "For Christ's Sake: Notes from Jesus and Other Sacred Clowns." The students asked the dean to kick you out.

**BRAD:** You shouldn't tell that story here. They may think I don't like religion.

**HILLARY:** Or they may worry you like it too much when they hear the way you shout and sing! Some people won't be able to get past our using the words "seiki" and "Jesus" in the same sentence. The truth is that you are a shaman in the traditional sense, yet you belong to no tradition. You grew up in country churches in the Midwest, became a Bushman doctor in Africa, a Balian healer in Bali, a captain of the holy spirit in St. Vincent, and Osumi Sensei's only heir to seiki jutsu, among other things. That's one of the reasons you delight me—you defy category.

**BRAD:** I just love God. When you defy category, you get closer to deifying glory!

**HILLARY:** I love your loving God. I'll never forget the time you woke up at two o'clock in the morning and got on your knees to pray. You asked for our lives to be led. Then your cell phone beeped right after your prayer ended, indicating that an e-mail had come in. When you went to see what message had come through, it started with "Dear Man of God."

**BRAD:** We were invited by more than a thousand African ministers who work with their poor congregations in over a dozen African countries, from Sudan to Uganda and the Congo, to come teach them how to enrich their relationship with spirit. That was amazing timing.

**HILLARY:** Just like this morning when we were in the Treme in New Orleans and went in that room where the Mardis Gras Indians were drumming and singing. The life force got a hold of us and made us feel close to Africa and all its original raw spirituality, overflowing with vitality and soul. How can we share spirited seiki with others who are looking for it but don't yet know what they are looking for?

**BRAD:** Perhaps we need to bring in the clowns to help those seiki hounds make some holy sounds. It's time for some tender howling, rather than the rough growling of know-it-alls.

**HILLARY:** Those Rumi love dogs do more than howl. They point to the moon.

**BRAD:** I didn't know that those were pointing dogs.

**HILLARY:** Sure, if you dream of a pointing dog, it can point you to a spiritual classroom.

**BRAD:** Are you clowning around?

**HILLARY:** Let me paint a frown and a tear on my face so I can be more ridiculously incongruent as I say with a smile, "That ain't it."

**BRAD:** Keep on saying, "That ain't it" over and over again until the questions and answers are silent.

**HILLARY:** When the chatter stops, you can say, "That's it!"

**BRAD:** Through contraries and crazy contradictions, you just might get William Blake to wake up again. Why don't we write a musical comedy about Blake?

**HILLARY:** Great, then you can sing, "The gods have a job for you: Go illustrate the book of Job."

**BRAD:** You are hilarious. I'm feeling ready for a seiki session now. Thanks for loosening up the space.

**HILLARY:** We have a client coming who said she just read our book. I see you are already bobbing and rocking. Let me sing you a little question, "What shall we say to the next person who pays for her life to be made of more than clay?"

**BRAD:** I think we should ask her why she only read the book. Did she put it in the freezer? Has she drilled a hole in it? Let's tell her to drill a hole in the book.

**HILLARY:** I can hear you saying, "If you don't have a power drill, find someone who has one. If you can't find a drill, find a way to drill through some of the pages, preferably all of the pages. You are to conduct this task with absolute seriousness, revering the possibility that so-called 'irrationality' may awaken what you have been seeking and open a door to a surprise that has been waiting to be discovered."

**BRAD:** And I can hear you adding, "Your cerebral cortex is tired and full of all those promising words that may have tried to inspire you—from shamanism to healing to feminism to Buddhism to quantum whatever—but arguably none of these words or their many meanings will actually make the needed difference. Let us attempt to take a journey into the center of the Earth, our inner landscape of the non-Jungian pre-primal unconscious, the analogic (non-digital) unknowable, the original formless full-bodied emptiness. Fasten your cognitive seat belt, close your book, and go look for a drill."

**HILLARY:** I recall the time we actually did this in a doctoral class we taught in San Francisco. We asked our students to drill a hole in their textbook, which was *Aesthetics of Change,* the book you wrote that is considered a classic in the science of cybernetics.

**BRAD:** We also drilled a hole through the book, wondering what we would find. We pretended to be lost, wondering about the mission of the class. We wrote out a simple request with a crayon, "Please help us find the direction to follow." Then we pushed our question through the book hole before we went to sleep. We agreed to wake up the next morning believing that our unconscious would deliver an answer.

**HILLARY:** Our only uncertainty concerned the form in which our answer would be delivered. Would it come inside a remembered or unremembered dream? Would it be in the form of a surprising feeling that takes place the next day, or in a book that is found while browsing at a library? We are always grateful for the way mystery may be unknowingly received when we grant it permission to reveal/conceal itself inside and outside understandings.

**BRAD:** This is a "needing to get more deeply lost before you can get significantly found" sort of thing.

**HILLARY:** Yes. Visualized or imagined drilling doesn't count. We're not just being witty. If you want seiki you gotta get gritty. This needs to be enacted. Come to think of it, if you've already read this book, you'll need to drill two holes before the second reading. That should be twice as potent.

**BRAD:** Yes, we mean it: go drill a hole in this book. Thinking about it or wondering about drilling the hole IS NOT a substitute for doing it.

**HILLARY:** If someone really wants seiki to flow from this book, what else could they do to open it up?

**BRAD:** Let us count the ways: underline spaces rather than words, talk to the book, place it on a serving plate at the dining table, play catch with it, add wheels to its back, create a different book cover, add your name to the author's to make it a collaborative writing/reading, glue a mirror to the front of the book, give your book a massage before reading, or run a string through the hole and floss it before reading.

**HILLARY:** You can place the book on top of your head and ask it to come down to the level of your heart before reading, move where you are sitting after reading each page so that your reading moves you around a circle, perform a naming ceremony—the book needs a name, not a title—give it a name that gives you the possibility for a more personal relationship with the book, or create a family history for the book.

**BRAD:** I'd like to see you write alternative chapter titles in colored ink under each black and white chapter, change male pronouns to a nonsense word like *zerp,* and write a fictitious author biography on the inside of the front cover.

**HILLARY:** I would be delighted to see you write a fictitious reader biography on the inside of the back cover, make a little cardboard or paper sack room for your book to sleep in at night—call it the book's private quarters, call someone and say that your book has something to say to them, or place your book in the funniest spot in your home.

**BRAD:** After your book has resided in a funny spot, carry it to a serious place and have it stare at the seriousness that needs loosening.

**HILLARY:** Attach a light to your book and place it under your bed for one night with the light on, purchase or make a mask for the book to wear, plug a power cord into your book and run the other end to your heart, like one of our clients did. Wonder whether the book is charging you with seiki or if it's the other way around.

**BRAD:** Write a letter to the tree that gave its life for the book.

**HILLARY:** Write a paragraph about whatever comes to mind and then randomly place it in the book, making it an unusual special edition. Take your book to a library so it may visit other friends and introduce the book to other books it may not know.

**BRAD:** Plan to mail the book to yourself—consider this a vacation for the book.

**HILLARY:** Encourage the book to have an out-of-body experience.

**BRAD:** Send out a press release describing the hole in your book and what is happening to it—try to make some news.

**HILLARY:** Finally, when you finish reading the book, have a "The End" party. But before you do any of these things, drill a hole in it.

**BRAD:** When you drill a hole in your book, you are making an "opening," giving the book an "eye," taking one step toward facing it, rather than defacing it. Or consider the hole a blowhole and squirt some water out of it. That makes a whale of a tale.

**HILLARY:** I have a story to share: In the beginning of human culture, people knew how to shake themselves into bliss and in so doing, the secrets of the universe were revealed. Then it all went to hell when we stilled our bodies and fed too many words to our minds. It's time for our seiki-filled bodies to write the next chapter.

**BRAD:** Look at the oldest library in the world—the rock art of southern Africa. What we see are images of people moving themselves into ecstasy. Many generations later, the elders of the oldest living culture on Earth today, the Kalahari Bushmen, still know that the electrified body inspired by heightened feelings and seiki—rather than anything remotely related to a calm and still presence—is the master key to being fully alive.

**HILLARY:** As the Bushmen say, words can trick us into believing anything. With word trickery, we may end up worshipping a pile of elephant dung or a heap of metal. Somewhere between the early cradle of civilization and the Internet, our species made the colossal mistake of proclaiming that words, theories, and understandings compose the road to salvation and happiness. This moved us out of the action stream and sat us down to "con-template." We became victims of innumerable template cons.

**BRAD:** If this is true, or even partially true, then it means that, with some exceptions, we have been misled for over a thousand years. The word games have led us to posit one form of gender, race, culture, nation, religion, or philosophy as superior to others—thereby justifying any and all acts of arrogant greed, war, and destruction of life and planet. Our born destiny is the same as the first human beings—to release our bodies, our whole beings, into feeling and expressing the deepest joy and ecstasy. In other words, dancing our selves on the seiki highway, going all the way to heaven, peace, and love.

**HILLARY:** If there is anything history teaches, it is that words and understandings aren't taking us anywhere but into more of the same quicksand. We must get tuned so we can hear what life is singing and bringing.

**BRAD:** It's time to turn to our species' deep collective past, held by the embodied wisdom expression of our shared ancestral culture. They teach us that the revolution we need cannot be voiced through lyrics or words, but through spirited rhythms and music.

**HILLARY:** Words only have value when they help liberate us from any overseriousness, either/or thinking, and any form of fundamentalism. We need a good Zen giggle and then a Kalahari wiggle.

**BRAD:** Unless the Dalai Lama and the pope are willing to trade costumes for a week and thereby truly contribute to the big breakup and meltdown of the differences that hurt others, they are unable to liberate us. We need to shake ourselves free from the shackles of stuck words and non-changing meanings.

**HILLARY:** What does it mean to sound the revolution? Can we offer a few teasers that provide some hints—while remembering that it can't be said in words?

**BRAD:** Recognize that whatever the great mystery is, it hates all reasonable and tamed definitions of god. God is not what the word authorities say it is! God is more of a rhythm, a song, and a dance, not a static concept.

**HILLARY:** We also need to put a warning label on so-called mindfulness practices, just like they do on cigarettes.

**BRAD:** Warning: Being relaxed and stilling the mind can put you to sleep when you need to WAKE THE DUCK UP!

**HILLARY:** There are too many spiritual quacks out there, and not enough people willing to be an ugly duckling for the holy.

**BRAD:** You only get to the deepest truth and the greatest vision if you paradoxically are wildly absurd and irreverent. Anyone wondering why we have been talking absurdly like this is definitely in need of more softening. Anyone loving this crazy wis-dumb talk may be ready to be shot by an arrow of seiki. ZAP! ZAP! Should we tell anyone that we eat Zapp's potato chips?

**HILLARY:** Did you realize that a spud without the letter *s* is a dud?

**BRAD:** I had forgotten, but let's not forget to tell everyone that there are NO kundalini accidents in the Kalahari. They only occur in cultures that sit like couch potatoes.

**HILLARY:** Our job is to get all those spiritual potatoes up and moving!

**BRAD:** I'll try not to rant about the so-called wisdom of the East that can be as ignorant as the wisdom of the West. Look where both have gotten us. Let's consider the wisdom of Mother Africa, the ancestral culture that honored rhythms more than words.

**HILLARY:** True. But let's not impose invented cultural categories on the direct experience of spirit or access to the holy. Seiki doesn't belong to any culture, color, gender, or geographic region. Neither does wisdom. Or idiocy.

**BRAD:** The revolution takes place through sounding it.

**HILLARY:** Is this revolutionary enough to inspire both a conversational turning and a spiritual burning?

**BRAD:** This is the revolution: fill the world with seiki. It's time to work the spirit, rather than talk about it.

**HILLARY:** I'm only interested in a revolution that *revolves*—a movement that is always moving!

**BRAD:** What a shame that the word *shaman* has lost its ecstatic meaning, given that shamanism is about the "technique of ecstasy." The old ones knew that shamanism is always a gift from the gods or spirits and not something that can be reduced to a weekend workshop.

**HILLARY:** We should reread Mircea Eliade, who noted in *Shamanism: Archaic Techniques of Ecstasy* that "one destined to shamanship begins by becoming frenzied."[1] How much frenzy are today's shamans experiencing?

**BRAD:** Eliade also underscored another important point we try to teach: "During his [or] her ecstasy the candidate sings shamanic hymns. This is the sign that contact with the beyond has been established.'"[2]

**HILLARY:** Going further, "If necessary, [the shaman] can drum, dance, and jump all night."[3]

**BRAD:** I like citing these quotations from Eliade's collection of quotations, which is essentially what his book was. What he cited seems to have been overlooked by many workshop-bred shamans. For instance, "This is the well-known sign of a genuine ecstatic experience: 'he feels as though he were drunk, and does not know whether it is day or night nor what he is doing.'"[4] Furthermore, "what differentiates a shaman [is] his ecstatic experience."[5]

**HILLARY:** Even Eliade got lost because he never experienced shamanic experience, but instead stayed at home and read other people's accounts of it. He did note, however, that "the Yukagir have two terms to designate the shaman: a'lma [from the verb 'to do'] and I'rkeye, literally 'the trembling one.'"[6] As you like to say, Brad, "If there is no trembling or shaking, there is no shaman."

**BRAD:** I actually first heard that from a Micmac tent shaker named Dave Gehue. He, as well as all authentic shamans, knows that medicine songs are "purely ecstatic" and "that the shamanic 'spirit language' not only attempts to imitate animal cries but contains a certain proportion of spontaneous creations presumably explained by pre-ecstatic euphoria and ecstasy itself."[7]

**HILLARY:** Furthermore, "we find that many sages, alchemists, and sorcerers 'went up to heaven.'"[8] Anyone who goes all the way with the vital life force ends up finding out about or directly experiencing the seiki line or rope to God.

**BRAD:** I once tried to explain to a man who promotes his own brand of shamanism that ecstasy is not a simple trance, but a highly energized experience that makes you tremble. He didn't know about or value trembling and shaking and thought that a trance that inspires a day-dream-like fantasy is what constitutes shamanism—what he and others call "shamanic journeying." In the same way that King James distilled the Bible to popular prose, a wisdom tradition is boiled down until it no longer has any Gnostic experience, wildness, or ecstasy left. Only a routine remains, and then people forget that the tastiest part of the apple isn't the core. Eliade similarly describes what happened to shamanism as it was corrupted by outsiders trying to reduce it to another method or understanding: "Hence we must conceive of Asiatic shamanism as an archaic technique of ecstasy whose original underlying ideology—belief in a celestial Supreme Being with whom it was possible to have direct relations by ascending into the sky—was constantly being transformed by a long series of exotic contributions culminating in the invasion of Buddhism . . . The phenomenology of the trance . . . underwent many changes and corruptions, due in large confusion as to the precise nature of ecstasy."[9]

**HILLARY:** Anything that talks about shamanism without serving the vital life force that makes one shake and tremble with ecstasy is not shamanism.

**BRAD:** Let's do something about it. Shall we ask people to conduct a shamanic experiment? Stay up two hours later than usual and wake up thirty minutes earlier than usual. Consider this a *shamanic interruptus*. As you stay awake for those two hours, say the words *teach me* over and over. Make sure you sing it while moving your body. Go outside and tell it to a star, even if there are no stars visible in the sky. Go to sleep believing that a shamanic change will be initiated by this action, whether or not it is revealed by vision. Expect it. Be grateful for it.

**HILLARY:** If you do this, you might go inside the jaws of a mythopoeic crocodile, rest peacefully in your grandmother's lap, find yourself with wings, talk with a honeybee, dance with a rose, dissolve into the soil, or become a steam of passion.

**BRAD:** You might make love with a grasshopper, enjoy breathing fire released by a dragon, dance on lily pads, give birth to your mother, marry a unicorn, ride a giraffe, enter the intestine of a lion, drink the blood of a turnip, talk to a dandelion, sprinkle yourself with letters, get baptized in laughter, or dive into a hole.

**HILLARY:** You might listen to yourself say what cannot be said or feel your heart crack open, as you are loved by the light, embraced by the unseen, and surrendered to the void.

**BRAD:** As you pledge allegiance to the wild, sing a joke, wrap yourself around a pencil, talk with your hand, heal 5,000 dolphins, release 500,000,000,000 molecules, plunge into the sun, flirt with the moon, and drown in chocolate.

**HILLARY:** Don't forget to add two extra fingers, kiss with your ear, write a letter to your next incarnation, receive a nut, and shout a silence.

**BRAD:** Let's tell all the seiki-less shamans that they should make a relationship with some fruit. In your imagination, create some pear bears, banana giraffes, apple owls, and grapefruit kittens. Until plants and animals have interactive relations in our minds, we cannot have nontrivial relationship with either. Go find your new fruit allies from the mytho-absurdo-poetic world.

**HILLARY:** Tell them the vision you had where you found a nest inside your head.

**BRAD:** I saw the top of my head as an egg that was cracked all the way across the top. When I touched it, the shell fell away to reveal a soft covering that still looked like an eggshell. It then broke open and four or five baby birds fell out, taking first steps as they tried to stretch their wings. I had no brains—the inside of my head was a bird's nest.

**HILLARY:** We can collectively build a nest. Each person can gather materials for a nest. Place it near or under your bed. Imagine that all of our gatherings will be watched by spirit, and held inside a very large nest. In this nest we shall place our special images, markings, words, metaphors, symbols, indications of relationship with other living presences, and our soul. There shall be a great hatching. Each of us is necessary to create the nest. Ask anyone with an open heart and imagination to join our cause. Prepare for the birth of a university. It will not offer any cool degrees. It will only offer the hottest degrees of seiki.

**BRAD:** Gathering the straw, grass, stones, threads, ropes, flower petals, words, symbols, metaphors, words, rock art, songs, fabric, buttons, seashells, branches, jars of fresh water, mud, clay: building our nest. Your mother was once your nest. Let us honor her by placing her name in the nest. Feel free to post the names of your grandmothers, real or imaginary.

**HILLARY:** It's not about shamanic ritual. It's about BEING shamanic/alchemical/transformative in all things. To shamanize yourself, CHANGE!

**BRAD:** Do you remember when we taught that group of eighteen- and nineteen-year-olds at a college? We only gave them one homework assignment: before you go to sleep, tape the holiest symbol you know to your belly button and the silliest symbol you can find to your tailbone.

**HILLARY:** Many of those students had spontaneous spiritual awakenings that night. They woke up shaking with bliss. It was miraculous!

**BRAD:** We would like for you to imagine that a major transformative experience will happen to you soon. It has already begun. Expect it to continue growing. Prepare for it to hatch. Start moving toward it as it is moving inside of you.

**HILLARY:** In the world of mystery, the place where shamans unlearn, we may cry for a vision, lament and beg for a song, and wait patiently for the gods to gift us in any way. Some of the greatest shamans have apprenticed for years, fasted for weeks, and sat through many ceremonies, waiting to receive seiki, or a life-force awakening. If you are waiting, then you are like all the shamans who have ever lived. You are journeying toward seiki, wondering how to make yourself more available for its entry.

**BRAD:** Why not, while conversing with someone, randomly say, *"rosa mystica"* in the middle of your sentence? If asked what it means, say this is an extremely rare mystical practice. Or wear a rose over your heart or on the top of your shoe or the top of your head.

**HILLARY:** Why not serve rose tea to a tree?

**BRAD:** Adopt a thorn.

**HILLARY:** Attach a stem to your pen and write a letter to yourself, explaining how you need to communicate with flowers.

**BRAD:** Purchase a rose at a flower shop. Then purchase a second rose at another flower shop. Introduce them to one another and escort them on a date.

**HILLARY:** Sleep on the floor next to your bed, while allowing a rose with its stem to sleep in your bed instead.

**BRAD:** Do all of the above again and again, but add at least one change each time.

**HILLARY:** The words wrapped around the everyday make things stick together, bound for no reason other than to stabilize the every of the everyday. Minding and wording are doing the gluing.

**BRAD:** Then we can assume that no one can possibly change without new minding or new wording, but that is just another minding and wording, more of the same gluing.

**HILLARY:** The way out—the transformative hinge, door, and exit—requires undoing the gluing, loosening the words and mind.

**BRAD:** We are here to help release the straitjackets that hold togethu. everyday habits, clichés, overused understandings, and homeostaticized realities.

**HILLARY:** Seek release from the karmic recycling of psychological re-re-re-re-re-incarnations. You may have to trick yourself, arrange an accident to fall outside the box.

**BRAD:** Do so with altered states of action. Begin by stepping into the world in a way that is out of step with the binds that restrain the world from being free, empty, and unready.

**HILLARY:** Blow a puff of wind. Announce the end of the habituated, predictable you. Reinvent your next life. Dress rehearsal tomorrow!

**BRAD:** Swallow any available seed and say, "It's time to grow."

**HILLARY:** Brad, please give us that prayer of yours.

**BRAD:** Lord, make us instruments of your divine madness. Make us empty so we can know the fullness of your original mysteries. Help us experience who we are not so we can become who we are. Help us be serious about the absurd, and absurd about the serious. Fill our bodies and minds with creative energy and inspired expression. Bring us contrary visions. We rejoice in being spiritual idiots, fools, and imbeciles completely devoted to your unattainable wisdom. We ask that seiki pour into our heart. For these things we pray. Amen.

**HILLARY:** Some will say that you, a wild seiki-bred shaman, should be seriously concerned about spiritual protection. But I see how you stand in the light, feel the love, and then get downright silly. That's a triple whammy: Evil hates light, love, and laughter. It can slip in only if one of those three guardians is not present. Of these three, perhaps the most powerful protection is the laughter of a child. Open your spiritual valves with shaking childish merriment. Then you will be ready and protected to do God's work.

**BRAD:** Lighthearted play also prepares us for serious sacred luminosity. The experiences of ecstatic energy and visionary rapture will take your breath away. Be serious about them, but only during the moments in which they occur. Afterward, return to levity. Forget forging the truth onto iron. Instead, be available time and time again for seiki to catch you, ride you, and fly you anew.

**HILLARY:** There are four sacred corners at the seiki crossroads: seiki, the ecstatic life force (or Holy Ghost power, kundalini, chi, n/om), spiritual vision, creative expression, and absurd experience. Never stay stuck in any one corner. Keep moving from one corner to another. This is the road you must stay on, and you must keep moving on it.

**BRAD:** The road is circular. It deepens, broadens, and heightens with each cycle you traverse. It is this virtuous cycle that fosters your growth in seiki, making you a part of the mythological Ouroboros, the dragon that chases its own tail in order to live a better tale.

**HILLARY:** Seiki loves all the religions of the world. This includes the unwritten religions and the unspoken traditions.

**BRAD:** Seiki asks us to pray with enthusiasm. Act out your desire to make a connection with holiness and the original spiritual mysteries. Without an enthusiastic enactment, it will be more difficult to open the mystical gates. Few enter the spiritual kingdom of the sacred here-and-now because few humble themselves to being a reborn child.

**HILLARY:** What is seiki? Where does it come from? What is its highest form? One word sums it up: love. Seiki is all about love. It is never about having power, being special, or getting magic. Love is what seiki serves—infinite and ever-expanding love in all possible forms and manifestations. Surrender to it and it will bring you the vitality of living through loving.

**BRAD:** Say "thank you" throughout each day and night. This is your mantra and secret saying. Be thankful for every breath and every experience. When you pray for guidance and later don't remember getting a big vision, say, "thank you," believing you received exactly what was perfect for you in that moment.

**HILLARY:** Let us remember what prophet John—we are speaking of John Cage—once said: "I have nothing to say, and I am saying it, and that is poetry."

**BRAD:** There is another performance he left us with, "Theatre takes place all the time, wherever one is, and art simply facilitates persuading one that this is the case."

**HILLARY:** You must be ready for an accidental performance to happen—which, according to Stravinsky, is the "only thing that can inspire us."

**BRAD:** Spontaneity is always an accident. It brings seiki. Seiki can't be faked. As you like to tease, Hillary, "one cannot fakey the seiki." Drill a hole. Make yourself a hollow tube, a sacred straw. Make room for the seiki to flow.

**HILLARY:** When the veneer is torn, even pricked with the tiniest drilled hole, the light will shine through. It will burn away all illusion and reveal the deepest felt love. Let it shine, let it shine, let it shine!

**BRAD:** Let there be nothing restraining us from entering infinite bliss. Honor the hole in your book and the holes in your life. Whatever has touched and pierced your heart has left you more ready for greeting the holy.

**HILLARY:** Consider this beginning list: seashell, roots, song, quark, kiss, distinction, creativity, God, god, chopstick, moon, drum, sex, galaxy, flea, ocean, dust particle, tremor, and locomotive. What does seiki have to say about these words and all the other words in every dictionary ever published?

**Brad:** In the seiki dreamtime, there is no importance given to the distinctions between the ocean and a dust particle or between the moon and a flea. Seiki launches a pilgrimage toward finding our flux-presence in the world as well as juggling/inventing/dancing/singing the galaxy inside a seashell, revealing the tremor we were born to embody.

**Hillary:** C. S. Lewis's devil advised his nephew in the matter of how to corrupt human beings: keep them thinking about the past and future. Never let them live in the present.

**Brad:** Seiki comes to reinstate the present. This is the dearest second coming. It is a present, a constantly transforming gift that never stops giving.

**Hillary:** The hole is waiting for you. Like Alice in Wonderland, jump into its open invitation. Holiness is rolling in this very moment, as its clouds gather in the sky. Prepare to be struck by lightning.

**Brad:** It's time to get ready for the spiritual classrooms. A new group of students is coming.

**Hillary:** Let's take them to heaven. The rope, ladder, and staircase are standing ready in our seiki room.

**Brad:** May the eternal delights and heavenly light shine upon all who are searching for the vital life force. We ask that a shower of blessings come to you, as we feel seiki is ready to transform your relationship with all that can bring wonder and love to your heart.

# APPENDIX

# ESSENTIALS OF SEIKI SELF-HEALING THERAPY

In 1928, Jozo Ishii of the Seiki Ryoho Kenkyu Jo (Seiki Treatment Institute and Research Establishment) in Japan published a book entitled "Essentials of Seiki Self-Healing Therapy." It is arguably the first written account of seiki jutsu. Ikuko Osumi Sensei gave a copy of this book to a few of her students. Some excerpts of this source text have been translated by Eric Houk and edited by Brad Keeney based on Osumi Sensei's commentary on the text. This is presented below to illustrate how seiki was discussed during the 1920s and 1930s in Japan.

What is seiki-healing therapy? This is when you use your own seiki vitality to stimulate the nerves in your body that have become weak, thereby causing spontaneous movement that heals. Then, relying on this, you can reinforce physiological action. As a result, if there is illness, the illness is cured. If there is pain, it is dispersed. In addition, a weak constitution is improved. A gloomy disposition becomes cheerful;

and not only does sluggishness become agile, most of the mental illnesses, including those barely helped by medicine, and most of the severe illnesses not treatable by conventional methods, are effectively healed as well. Even for those people who are perfectly healthy every day, using the seiki vitality practice restores mental and physical fatigue, and they become full of energy and great wisdom. If people who work as government employees, teachers, or other various occupations use it between work, they can release their fatigue right before their eyes during a break and improve their efficiency afterward. If students use this as part of their daily routine, they won't suffer with tiredness and will develop greater abilities. Seiki-healing therapy works by letting the body's natural healing process save and strengthen itself through circulating seiki as the body spontaneously moves.

At its core the seiki exercise is a positive and robust method of disease prevention, and if applied at home, the sufferings caused by illness can be avoided. Older people needing more mental and physical vitality can also use this method of movement to improve their lives. If used to treat the discomfort that results from physical disorders, one will return to normal before long, improve health, and prolong life. This is the great efficacy of seiki vitality.

The physiological reflex underlying the seiki practice is a fairly simple thing to acquire, but it cannot be achieved immediately. It must be cultivated over time. As the body and nervous system are gradually trained, the ability to provide excitation increases. When the practice is learned, the simple body reflex action takes place naturally. . . . With the seiki exercise, pain can quickly leave, fevers rapidly decline, and swelling gradually disperse.

As we more fully understand how seiki brings vitality to the human body, we become astonished by its great efficacy and immeasurable blessings. We must enthusiastically put it to practical use. More serious scholars and medical scientists are now researching seiki as we are in our laboratory.

Seiki can be called a pure spirit that refers to the god of infinite power in Western philosophy. It can also be called the unitary spirit of the universe, integrating the universe of power found in both the East and West. Seiki underlies the creation of all things.

Seiki—the vital force of the universe—is integrated in the universe as one power. I have studied seiki in the human body. To really comprehend seiki we must first understand the vitality of the universe. Understanding the vitality of the universe can help us account for the general vitality of the earth and help remove the mystery concerning the vitality of the human body.

Seiki vitality is the essence of life. It is the energy that occurs within the human body, and it exists in some form within all living beings. Even though scholars have named it "animal electricity," it is not simply electricity nor is it the frictional electricity produced by the movement of cells. The vitality of the human body also holds mystical wisdom and constitutes something different from the vitality of other animals. It is therefore necessary to think of the seiki vitality of the human body as differentiated from the vitality of other animals.

Seiki is more than a natural, reflex-like motion of the body. It can activate the hands to press and rub various parts of the body in the spontaneous self-treatment of disease.

Seiki in its intense form is most often perceived around the head more than any other part of the body. It can radiate light overhead as we see in the rings of light over historically known religious figures. For people who have a remarkable spiritual being and are full of seiki, vitality surges from their whole body and may appear to sensitive observers as a flame that emanates from the body.

Even though the teaching of seiki began during ancient times in the southern seas of the East and West, the power of science is still insufficient to fully study and explain it. It isn't the right time to scientifically understand it. However, our ability to use seiki vitality treatment isn't limited by the knowledge that science can acquire.

Seiki has a power of attraction. A seiki master can influence another person's body movement and health. For example, a seiki master can influence the posture of another person standing in front of him. Seiki emanates from the fingertips, and here we find that the hands and fingers are the main ways seiki is transmitted.

People with strong seiki will feel this influence the most. They are readily moved by the hands of another person using seiki on them. In addition, sensitive people can feel seiki. Particularly, women and children are somewhat more sensitive, and people who are oversensitive due to illness will feel it strongly.

In my introductory lectures on seiki, I address the people who say they know absolutely nothing about seiki vitality. I ask them to stand. Then I aim my fingertips toward their backs. I start doing small vibrations with both hands right away and this results in their shoulders moving. If they resist the power of seiki pulling them backward, the spinal cord clearly will curve backward anyway. These people often note the occurrence of a hot sensation in their backs.

Pointing the fingertips at each part of the body as I send seiki can determine the strengths and weaknesses of nerves, the presence or absence of paralysis, the presence or absence of disease, and so forth. Thus, for people with a stiff waist, the waist will resist the power of attraction; for those with a bad leg, the leg will resist; and in the case of spinal nerve paralysis, the resistance in that part of the spinal cord will be strong. . . . We can easily cause self-movement in people with illnesses that will help them heal.

When you have worked with seiki, you can experiment with this force on yourself. Take one of your own palms and aim it at the fingertips of the other hand. With sufficient seiki, it will radiate vitality and gradually cause them to move. This will cause a kind of sensation in the part of the palm that is facing the fingertips. Next, put both palms facing each other and quietly open and close them without changing the distance. At this time, you will feel a chilly breeze in the middle that is the force of seiki vitality.

We can perform self-movement experiments with the strengths and weaknesses of another person's seiki. The following method is used.

Both persons sit or stand while facing each other with their eyes closed. One person gently extends a hand and raises it high without exerting power on the whole body, and the other person gently extends a hand horizontally. . . . At a certain time through the natural power of attraction that seiki exerts, the weaker person will find himself pulled toward the stronger person. If the person with the horizontally placed hand is stronger, the higher placed hand of the other person will gradually go down. . . .

Most importantly, seiki vitality is an extremely spiritual thing.

# NOTES

## CHAPTER 1.
### INTRODUCTION TO SEIKI

1. Keeney, *Shaking Medicine,* ii.
2. Keeney, *The Bushman Way of Tracking God.*
3. Keeney, *Ikuko Osumi, Sensei,* 67.
4. Ibid., 51–52.
5. Ibid., 76.
6. Keeney and Keeney, "Seiki Jutsu."

## CHAPTER 4.
### THE DAILY SEIKI EXERCISE

1. Herrigel, *Zen and the Art of Archery,* 35.
2. Ibid., 47–48.
3. Palmer, ed., *A Jazz Odyssey.*

## CHAPTER 5.
### THE ENERGIZED BODY:
### USING SPONTANEOUS MOVEMENT TO HEAL

1. Morgan, *T.T.T.,* 68.
2. Fulford, *Dr. Fulford's Touch of Life,* ix.

## CHAPTER 6.
## SEIKI CONVERSATION:
## THE NEW FUTURE OF THE TALKING CURE

1. Tosches, *Where Dead Voices Gather,* 135.

## AFTERWORD.
## A CONVERSATION ON JUGGLING
## ZEN, JAZZ, AND SEIKI

1. Eliade, *Shamanism,* 16.
2. Ibid., 19.
3. Ibid., 28.
4. Ibid., 100.
5. Ibid., 107.
6. Ibid., 245.
7. Ibid., 440.
8. Ibid., 449.
9. Ibid., 507.

# BIBLIOGRAPHY

Eliade, Mircea. *Shamanism: Archaic Techniques of Ecstasy.* Princeton: Princeton University Press, 1964.

Fulford, Robert C., with Gene Stone. *Dr. Fulford's Touch of Life: The Healing Power of the Natural Life Force.* New York: Pocket Books, 1996.

Herrigel, Eugen. *Zen and the Art of Archery.* New York: Pantheon, 1953.

Ishii, Jozo. "Essentials of Seiki Self-Healing Therapy." Japan, 1928.

Keeney, Bradford. *Brazilian Hands of Faith.* Philadelphia: Ringing Rocks Foundation, 2003.

———. *Bushman Shaman: Awakening the Spirit through Ecstatic Dance.* Rochester, Vt.: Destiny Books, 2005.

———. *The Bushman Way of Tracking God.* New York: Atria Books, 2010.

———, ed. *Ikuko Osumi, Sensei: Japanese Master of Seiki Jutsu.* Philadelphia: Ringing Rocks Press, 1999.

———. *Kalahari Bushman Healers.* Philadelphia: Ringing Rocks Press, 1999.

———, ed. *Ropes to God: Experiencing the Bushman Spiritual Universe.* Philadelphia: Ringing Rocks Press, 2003.

———. *Shakers of St. Vincent.* Philadelphia: Ringing Rocks Press, 2001.

———. *Shaking Medicine: The Healing Power of Ecstatic Movement.* Rochester, Vt.: Destiny Books, 2007.

Keeney, Bradford, and Hillary Keeney. *Dancing on the Rope to God: The Moving Religion of the Ju/'hoan Bushmen.* (in preparation).

———. "Seiki Jutsu: Transformation and Healing through Spontaneous Movement." *Dance, Movement, and Spiritualities,* 1, no. 1 (2014).

Morgan, Doug. *T.T.T.: An Introduction to Trance Dancing.* Lantzville, British Columbia: Ship Cottage Press, 1988.

Osumi, Ikuko, and Malcolm Ritchie. *The Shamanic Healer: The Healing World of Ikuko Osumi and the Traditional Art of Seiki Jutsu.* Rochester, Vt: Healing Arts Press, 1988.

Palmer, Richard, ed. *A Jazz Odyssey: The Life of Oscar Peterson.* New York: Continuum, 2002.

Sanford, Agnes. *The Healing Light.* New York: Ballantine, 1983.

Tosches, Nick. *Where Dead Voices Gather.* New York: Back Bay Books, 2002.

Williams, George. *Religions of the World: Shinto.* Philadelphia: Chelsea House Publishers, 2005.

# INDEX

# BOOKS OF RELATED INTEREST

**Shaking Medicine**
The Healing Power of Ecstatic Movement
*by Bradford Keeney*

**Vibrational Medicine**
The #1 Handbook of Subtle-Energy Therapies
*by Richard Gerber, M.D.*

**Self-Healing with Breathwork**
Using the Power of Breath to Increase Energy and Attain Optimal
Wellness
*by Jack Angelo*

**The Power of Ecstatic Trance**
Practices for Healing, Spiritual Growth, and Accessing the Universal Mind
*by Nicholas E. Brink, Ph.D.*

**Ecstatic Healing**
A Journey into the Shamanic World of Spirit Possession
and Miraculous Medicine
*by Margaret De Wys*

**The Complete Book of Traditional Reiki**
Practical Methods for Personal and Planetary Healing
*by Amy Z. Rowland*

**Reiki for the Heart and Soul**
The Reiki Principles as Spiritual Pathwork
*by Amy Z. Rowland*

**The Five Tibetans**
Five Dynamic Exercises for Health, Energy, and Personal Power
*by Christopher S. Kilham*

INNER TRADITIONS • BEAR & COMPANY
P.O. Box 388
Rochester, VT 05767
1-800-246-8648
www.InnerTraditions.com

Or contact your local bookseller

1.) Sit on Wooden Stool at set Time  >  P. 74 Press Eyeballs

2. Prayer 197

3) Press Eyeballs gently P. 74

ENERGY
5 All There I
5 ACTIVATED 6

4) Sounds Movements (10) Poetic Rhyme (13) > 11-12 Masters - 13 Honey Like

91 - Begin where u end (P.2) Life
    (2) Feel heat (7) feel — —
    (29) hands
    (33) Initiation (34)            (24) White Snake —
    (38#) 39 - Stream of Honey Substance   26-27 LIGHT - Move Wave
    47 Seiki feeds on Love
    63 Ready

(42) You Must Experience IT
    (43) A MASTER connects [Seiki lines]
         Connects ALL (Vital Life Force)
    87 - Step 3

75 DAILY
Communication
(9) Uncon.
(15) purpose > To Hold / Promote
              VITAL LIFE FORCE                MASTERS
                                              30 Reborn

                                              82 EINSTEIN

Mind
52-53 Tricky

(171) If you love God - Seiki will flow
      If you Love Seiki - Then God will show